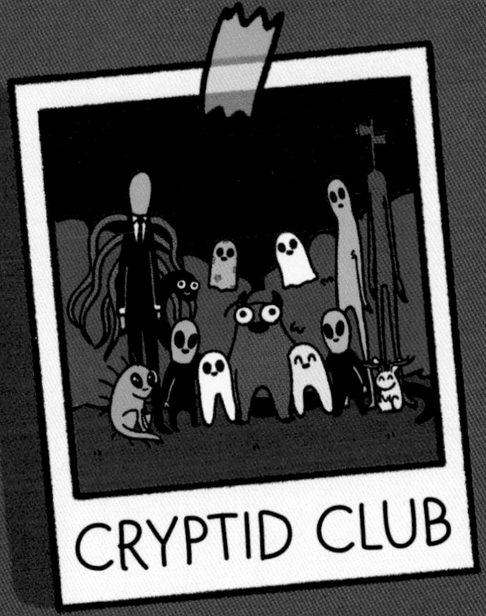
CRYPTID CLUB

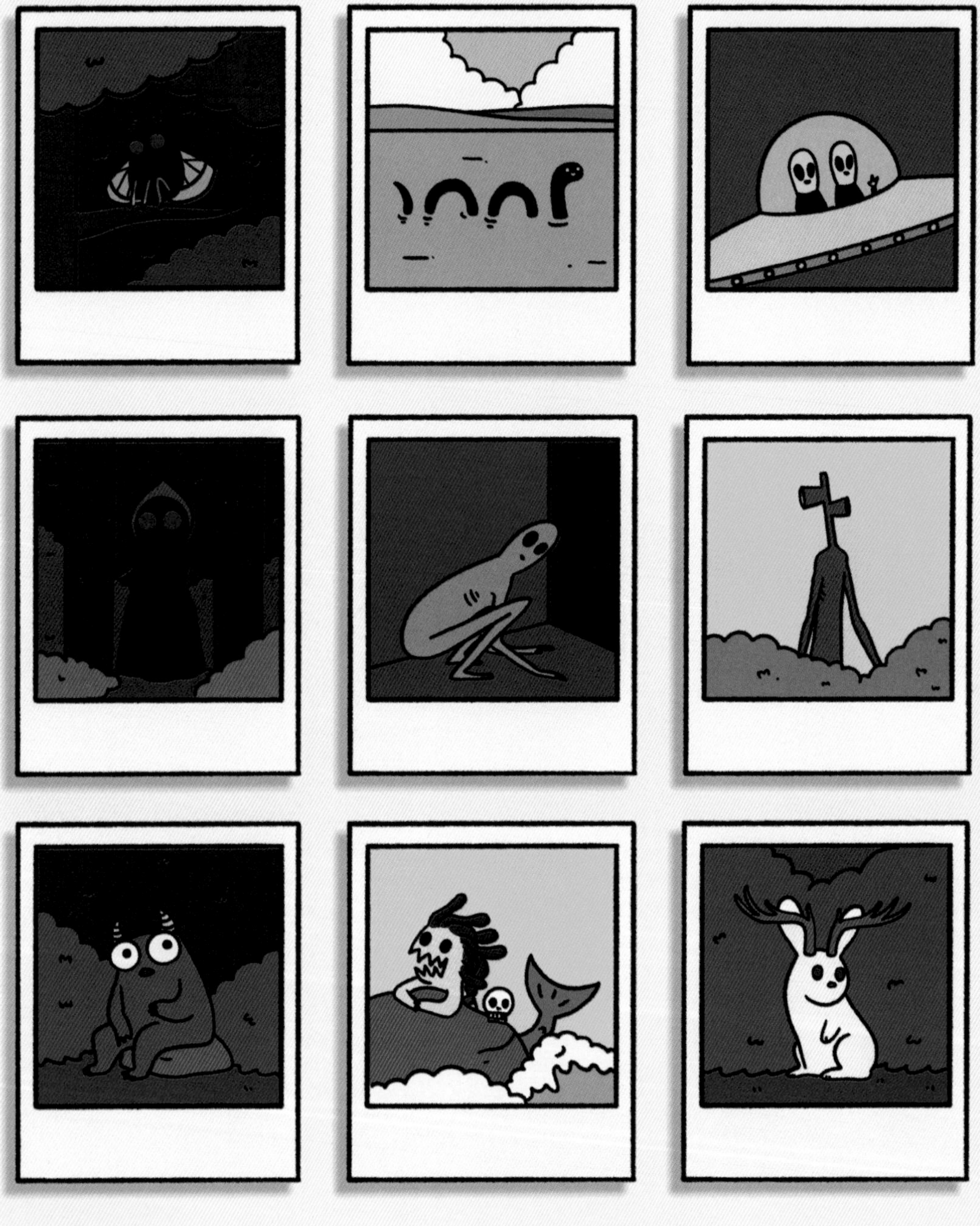

CRYPTID CLUB

SARAH ANDERSEN

Andrews McMeel
PUBLISHING®

The character of Siren Head
was created by Trevor Henderson.

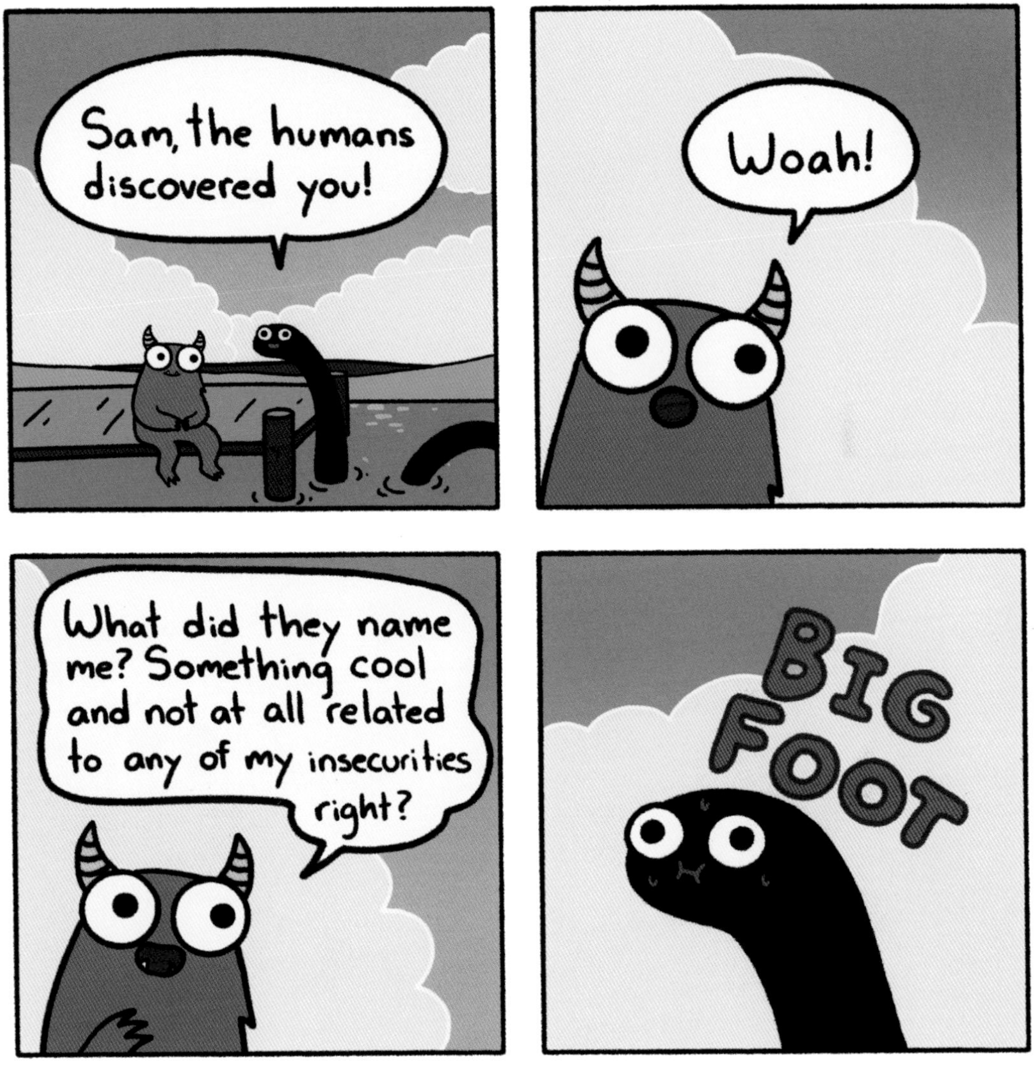

Sam, the humans discovered you!
Woah!
What did they name me? Something cool and not at all related to any of my insecurities right?
BIG FOOT

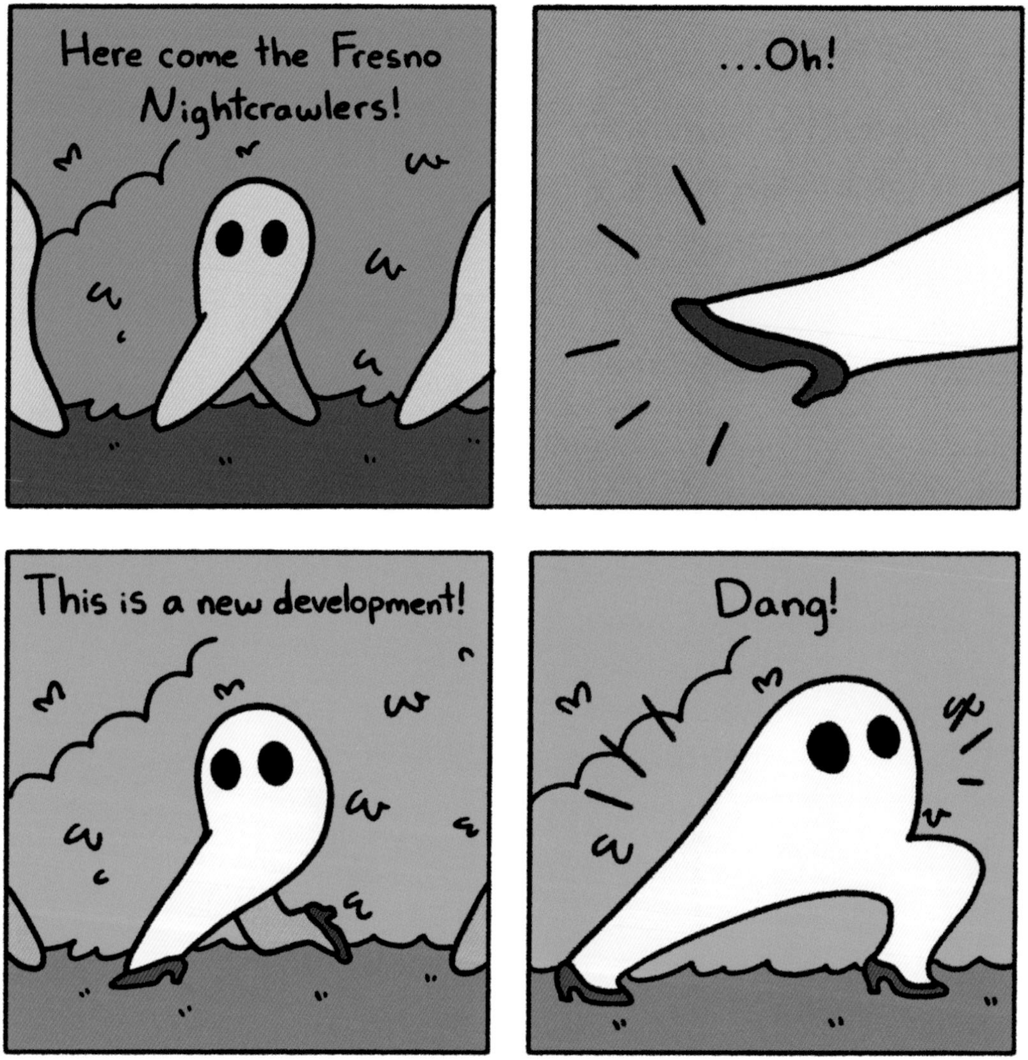
Here come the Fresno Nightcrawlers!
...Oh!
This is a new development!
Dang!

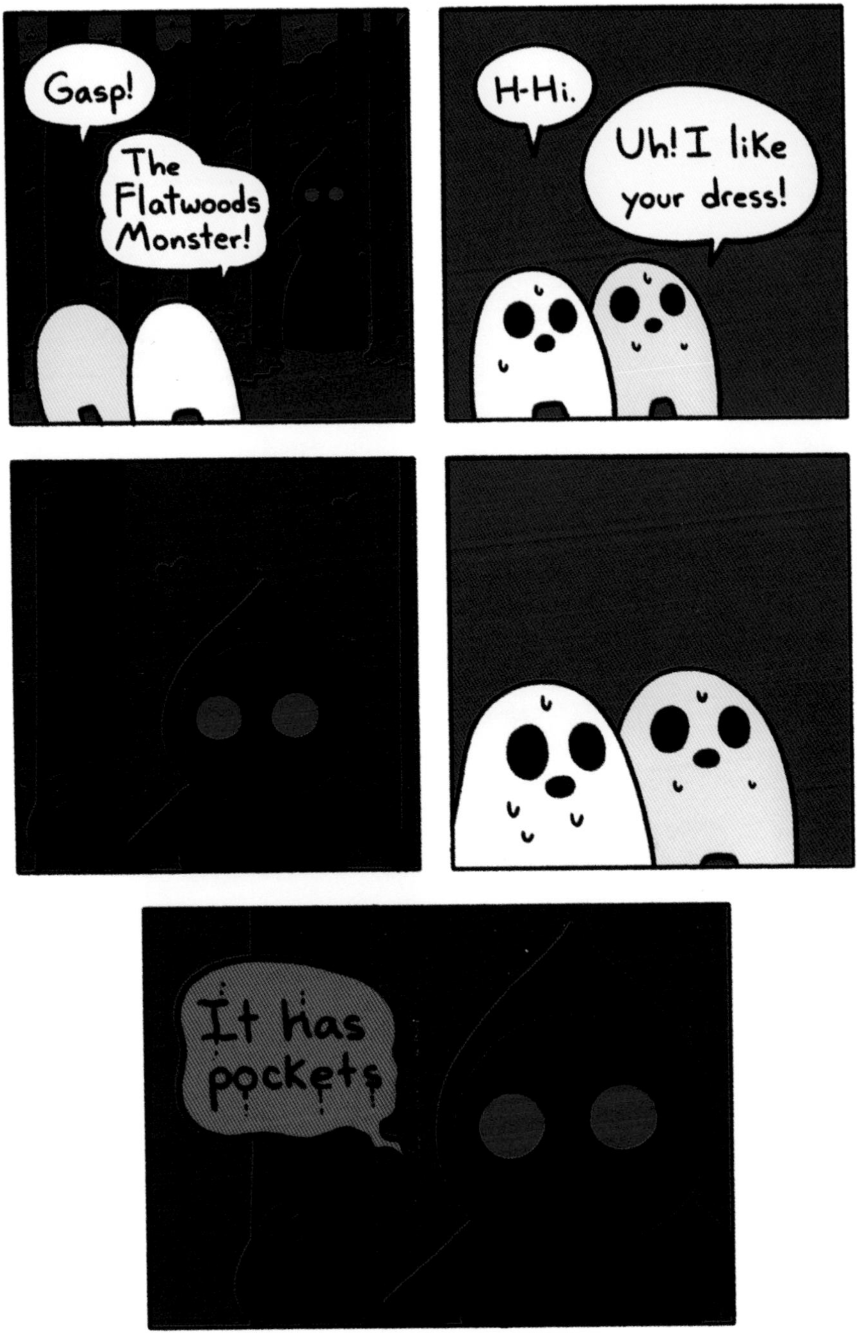
Gasp!
The Flatwoods Monster!
H-Hi.
Uh! I like your dress!
It has pockets

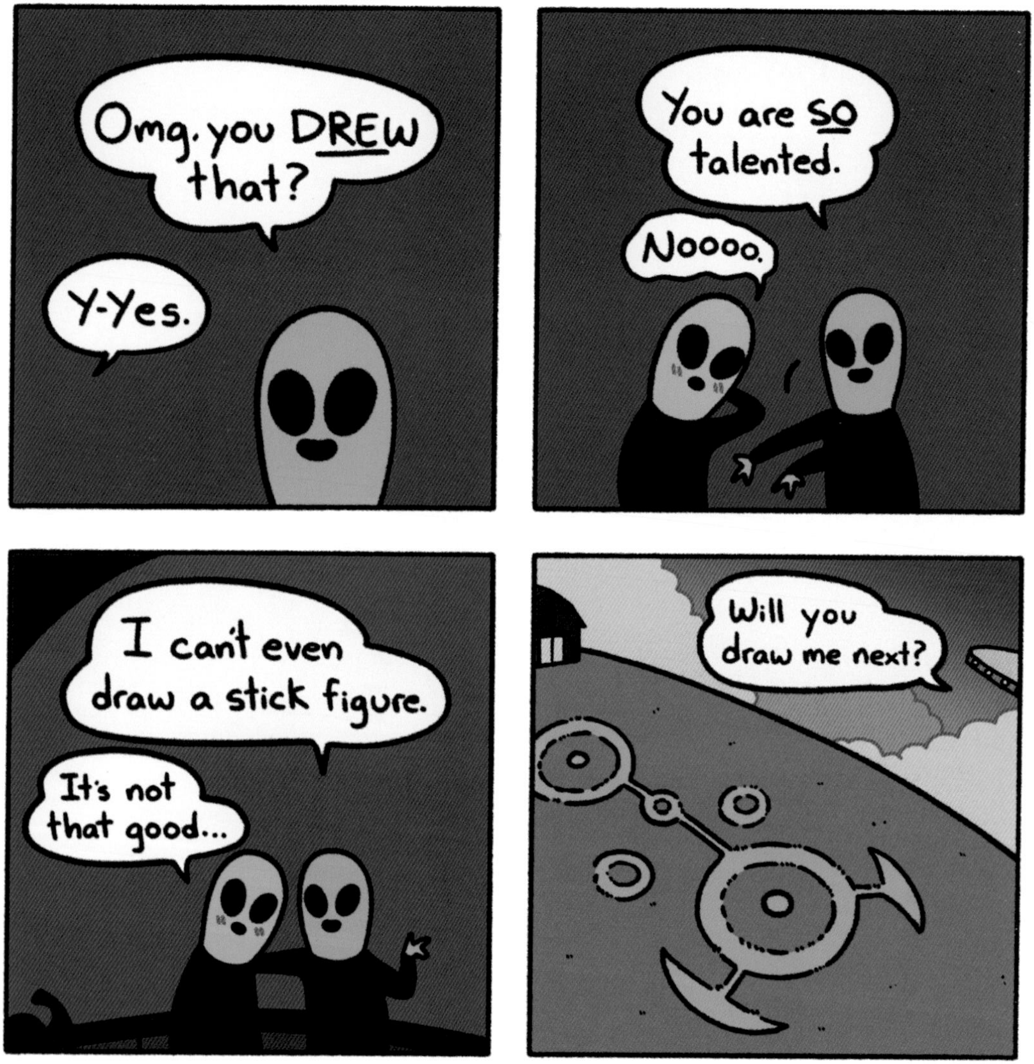

Omg, you DREW that?
Y-Yes.
You are SO talented.
Noooo.
I can't even draw a stick figure.
It's not that good...
Will you draw me next?

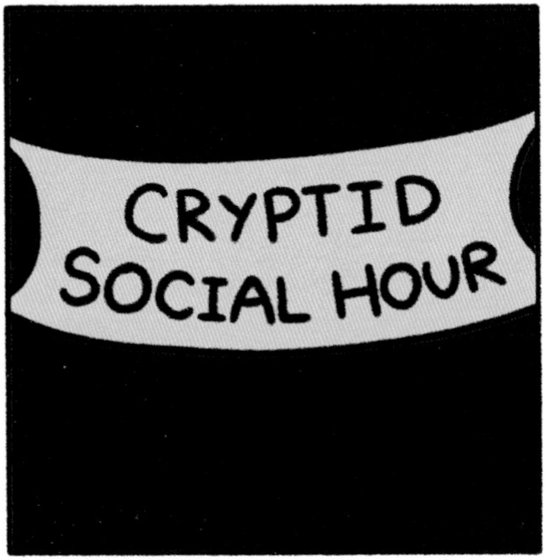
CRYPTID
SOCIAL HOUR

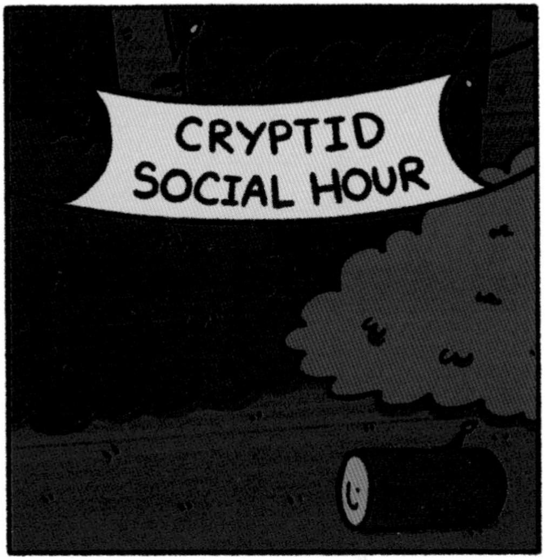
CRYPTID
SOCIAL HOUR

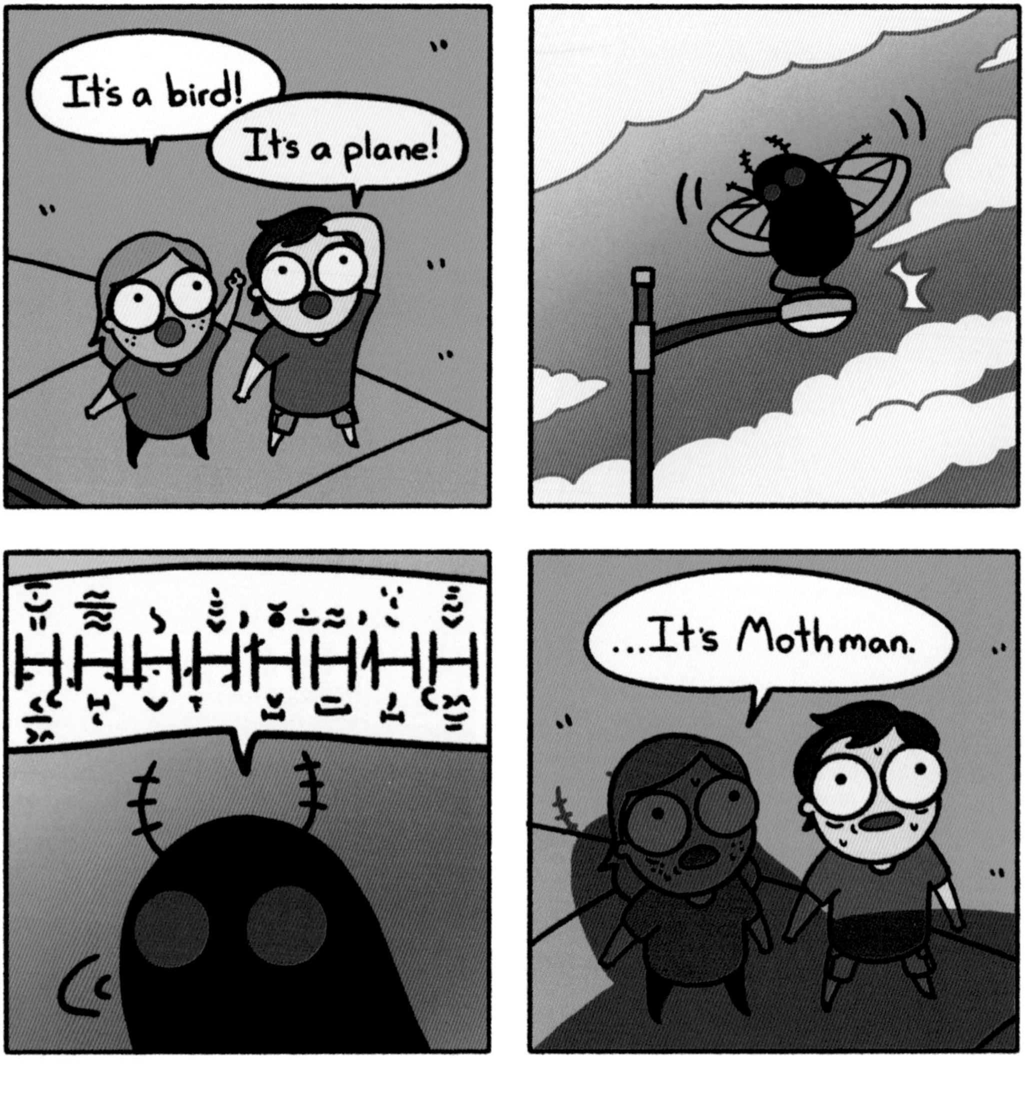
It's a bird!
It's a plane!
HHHHHHHHHHH
...It's Mothman.

UNFINISHED BUSINESS

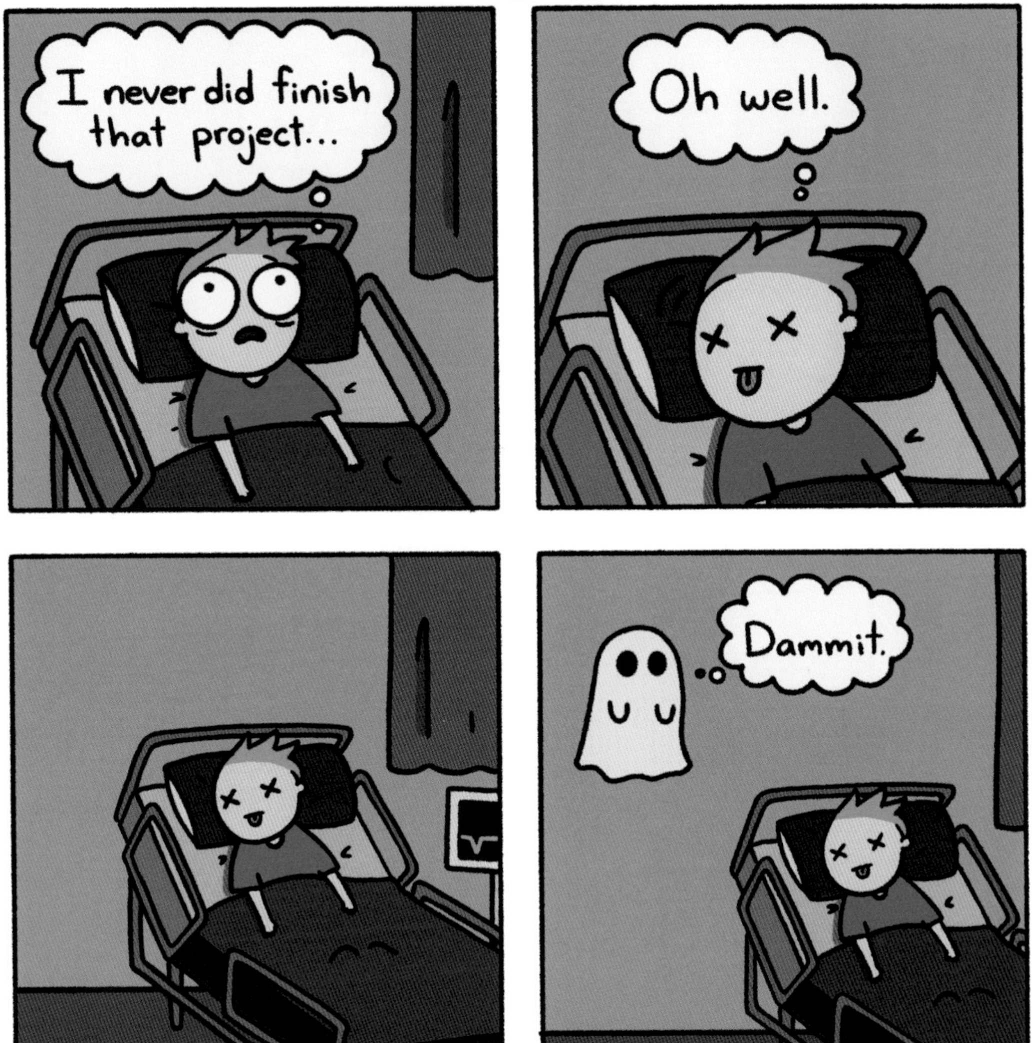
I never did finish that project...
Oh well.
Dammit.

RELEASE THE KRAKEN!
You're staying in time-out, Benjamin.

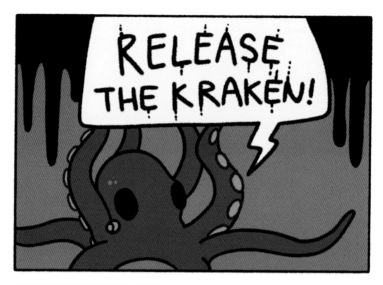

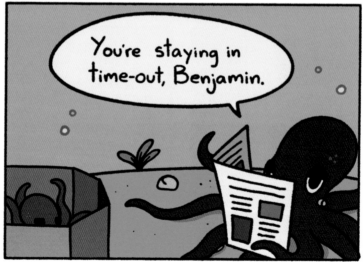

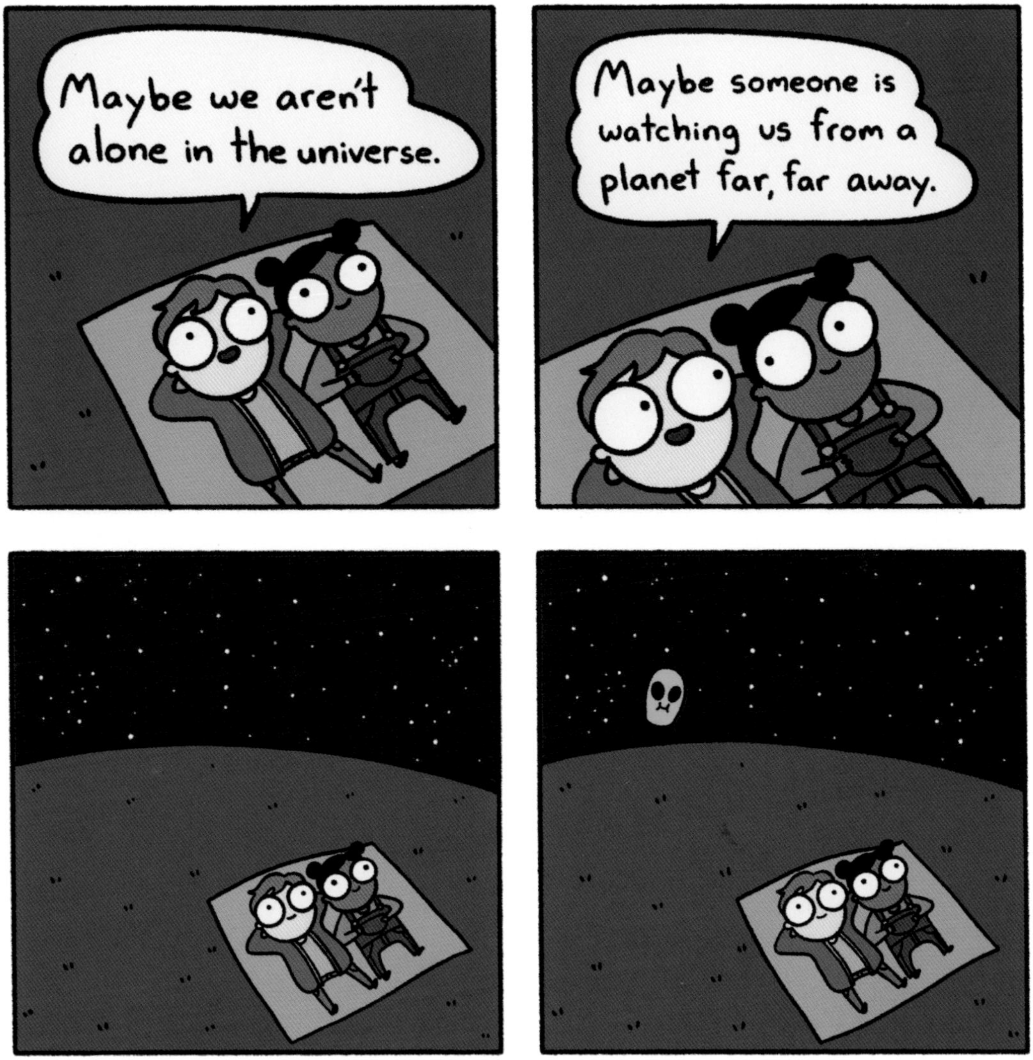
Maybe we aren't alone in the universe.
Maybe someone is watching us from a planet far, far away.

SLENDER MAN

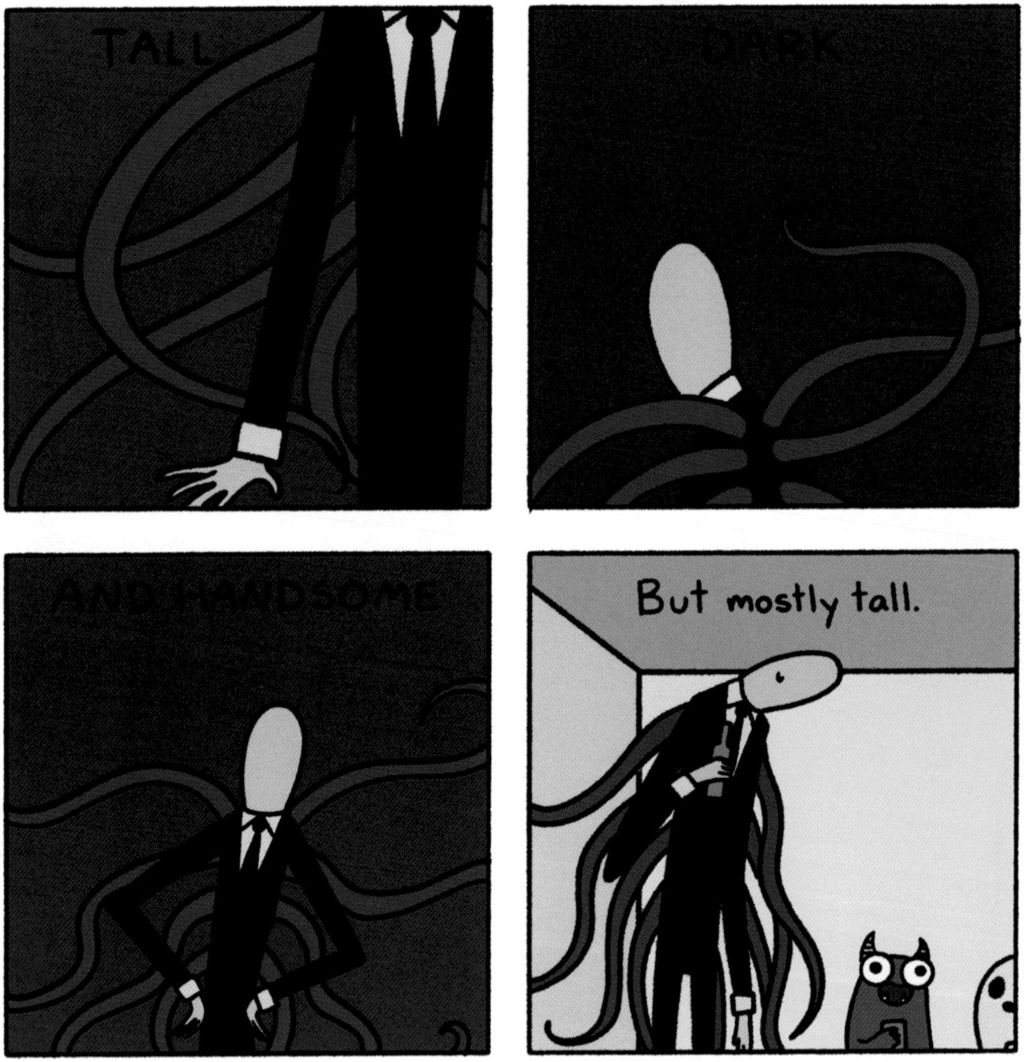
TALL
DARK
AND HANDSOME
But mostly tall.

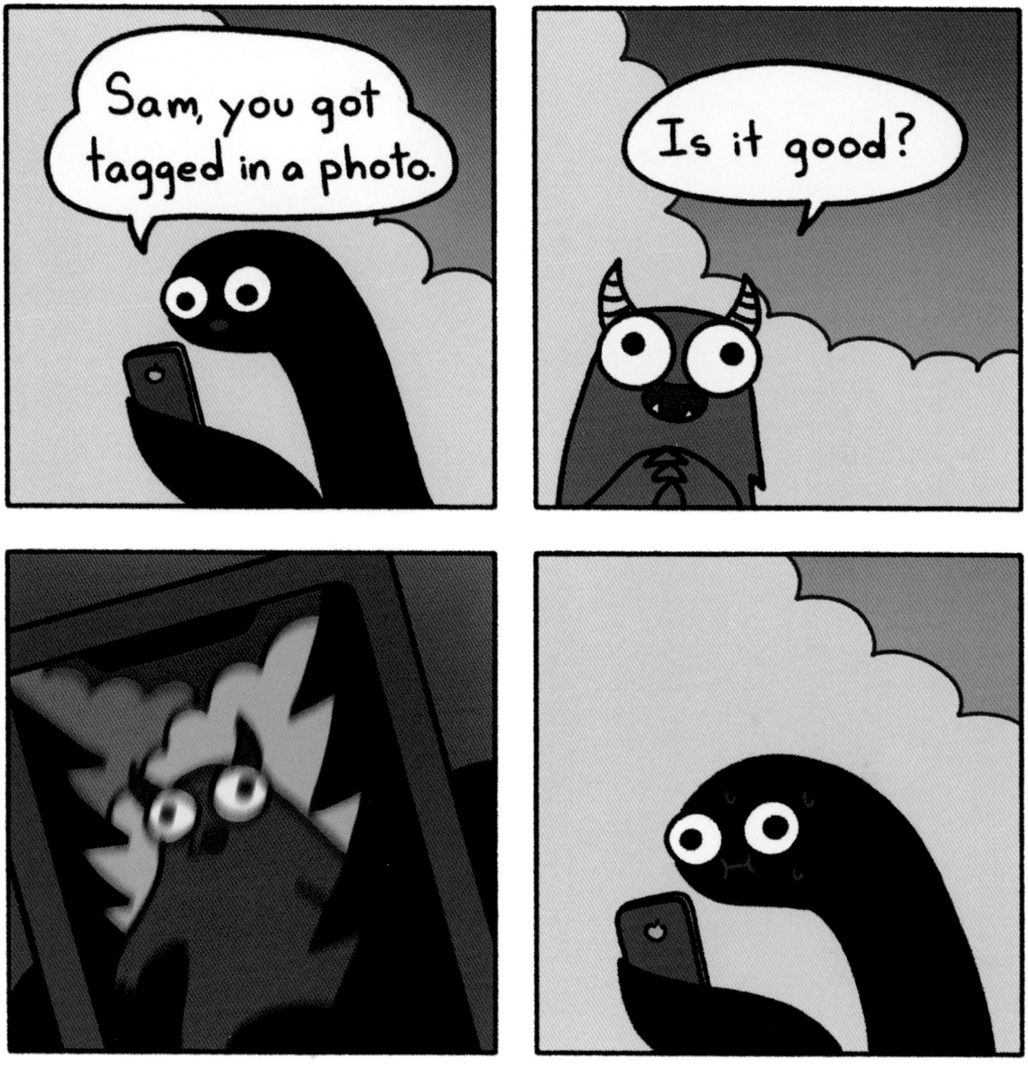
Sam, you got tagged in a photo.
Is it good?

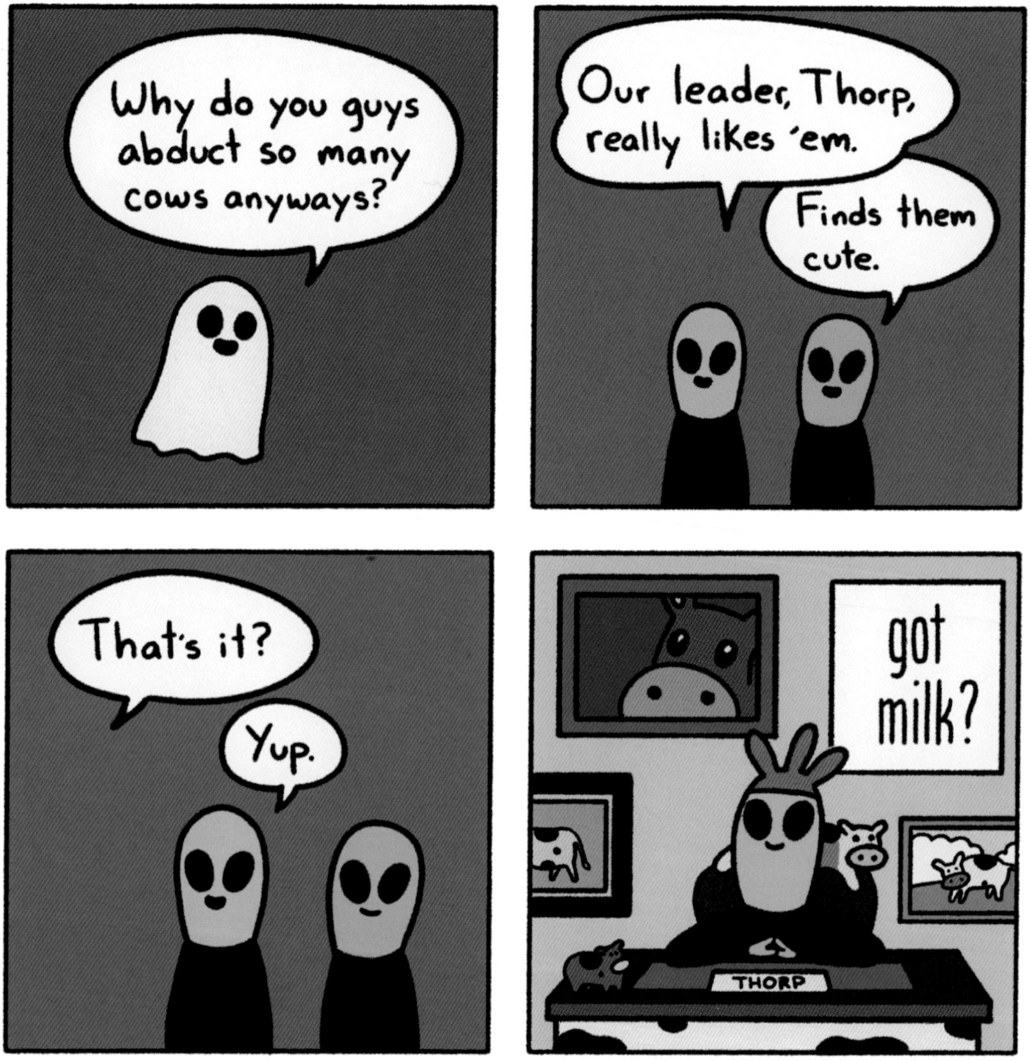
Why do you guys abduct so many cows anyways?
Our leader, Thorp, really likes 'em.
Finds them cute.
That's it?
Yup.
got milk?
THORP

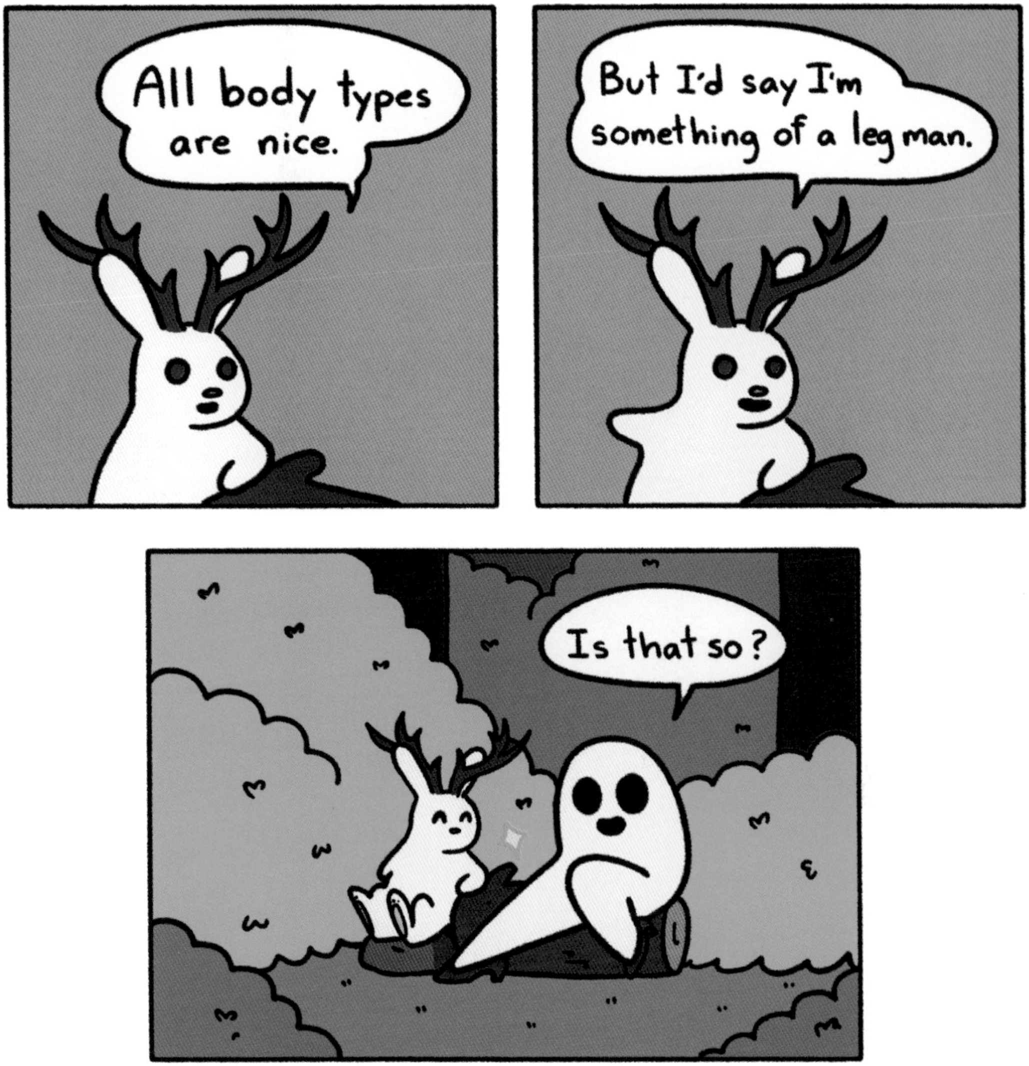
All body types are nice.
But I'd say I'm something of a leg man.
Is that so?

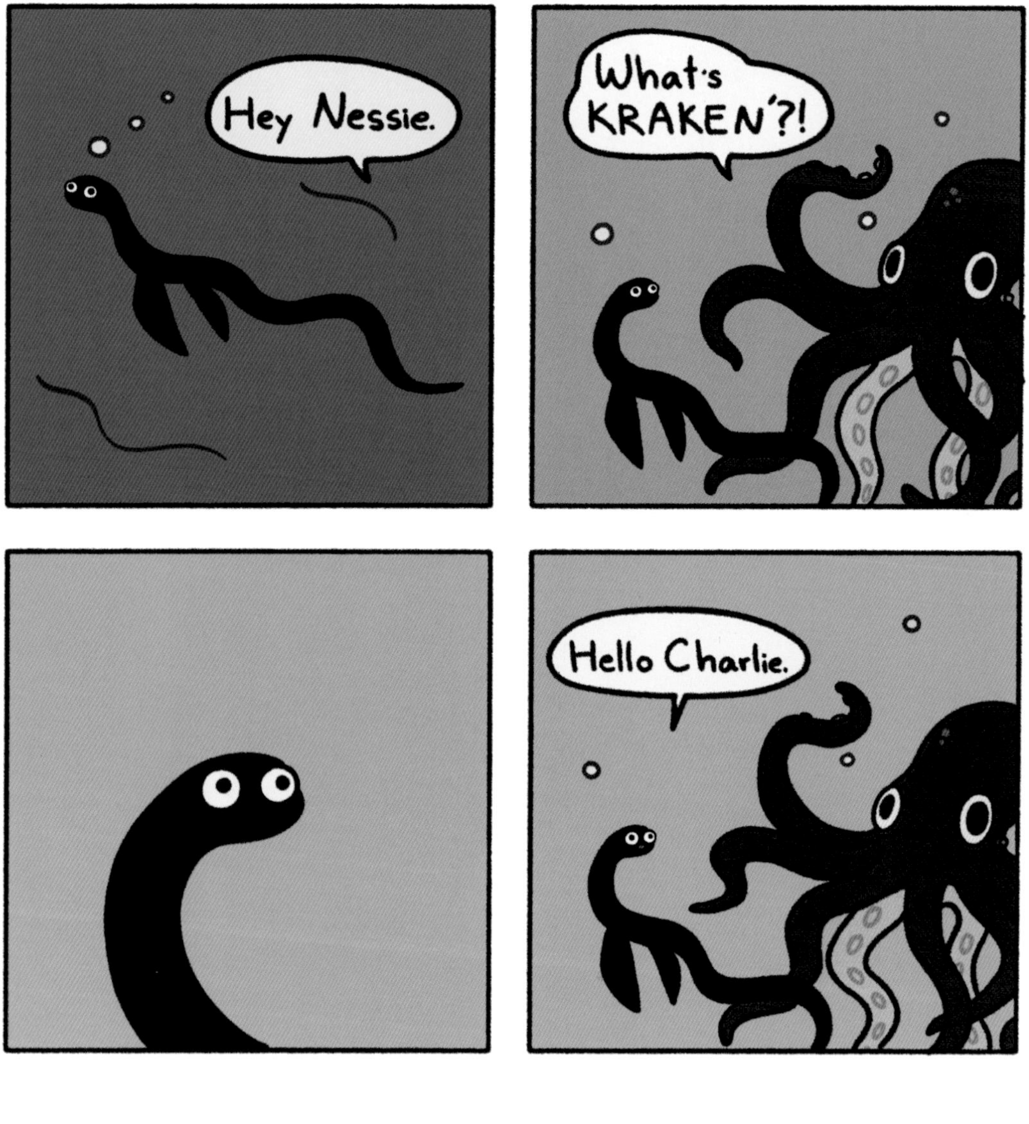
Hey Nessie.
What's KRAKEN'?!
Hello Charlie.

SLEEP PARALYSIS DEMON

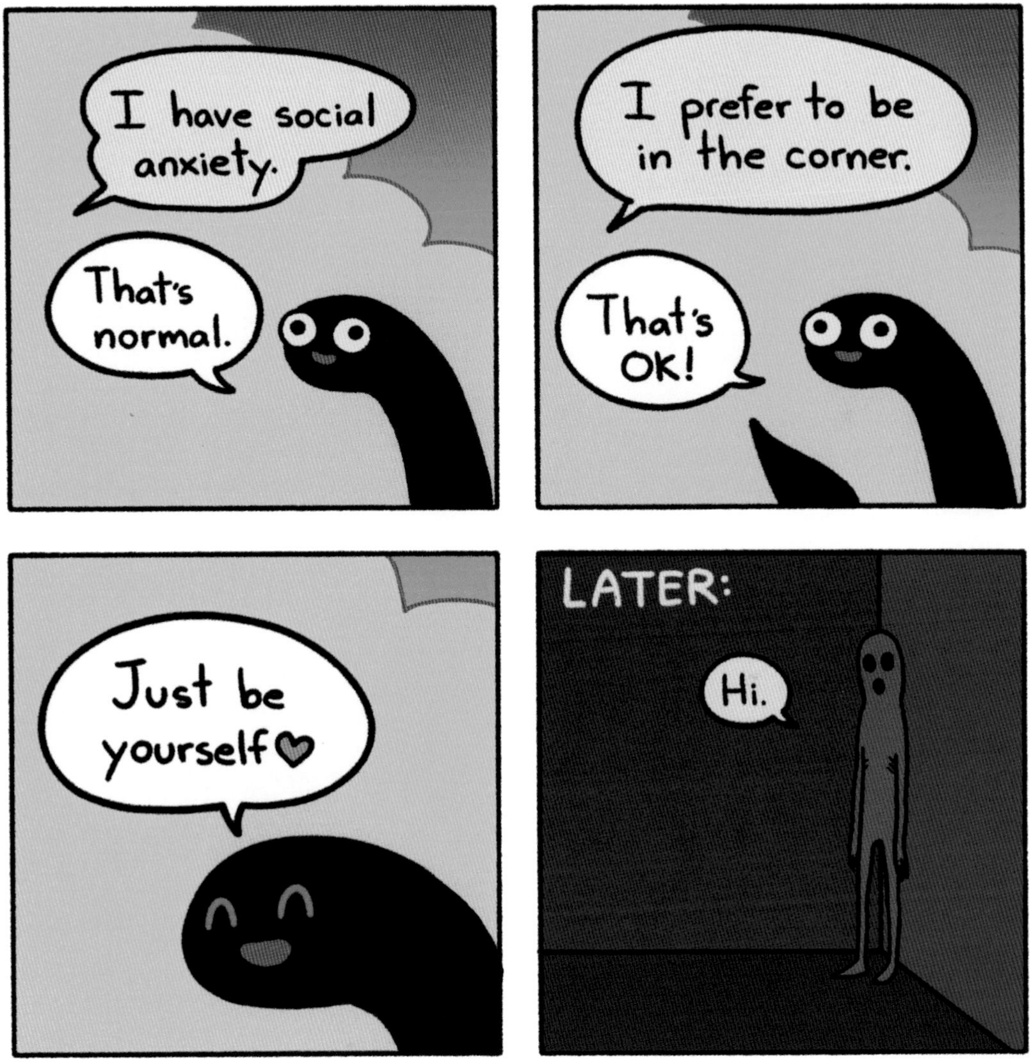
I have social anxiety.
That's normal.
I prefer to be in the corner.
That's OK!
Just be yourself
LATER:
Hi.

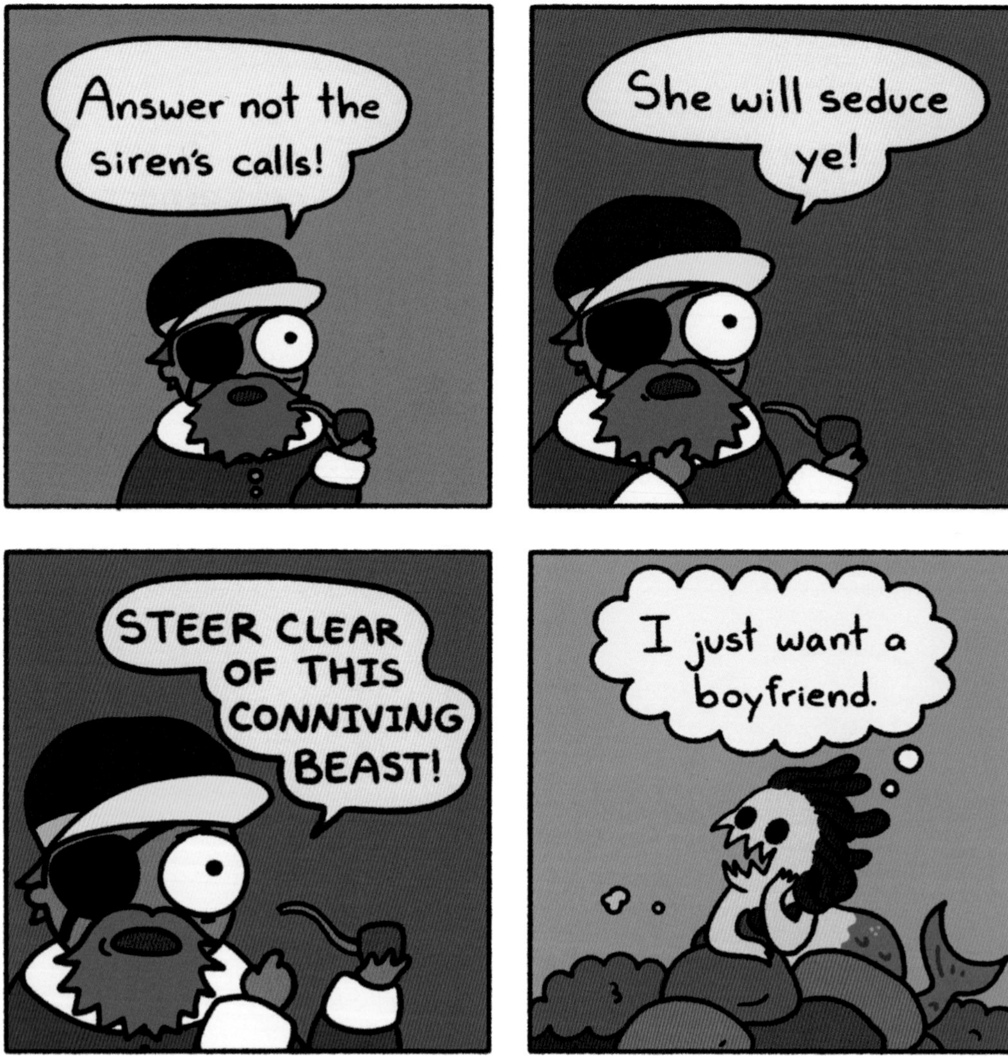
Answer not the siren's calls!
She will seduce ye!
STEER CLEAR OF THIS CONNIVING BEAST!
I just want a boyfriend.

CHUPACABRA:
THE FEARSOME GOAT BLOOD SUCKER

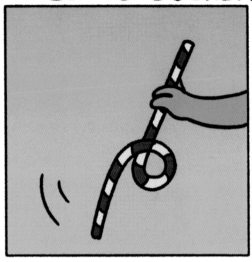

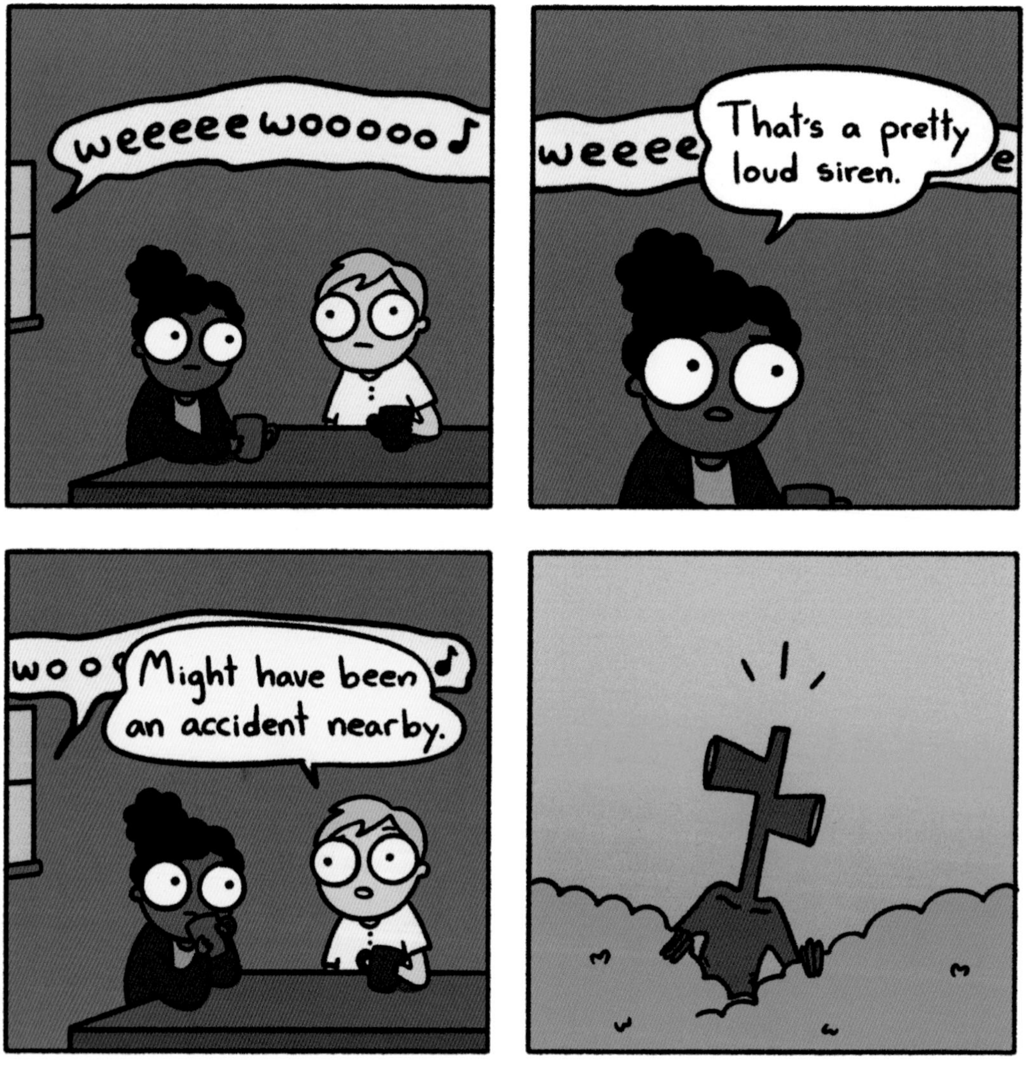
weeeeewoooooo ♪
weeee
That's a pretty loud siren.
e
wooo
Might have been an accident nearby.
♪

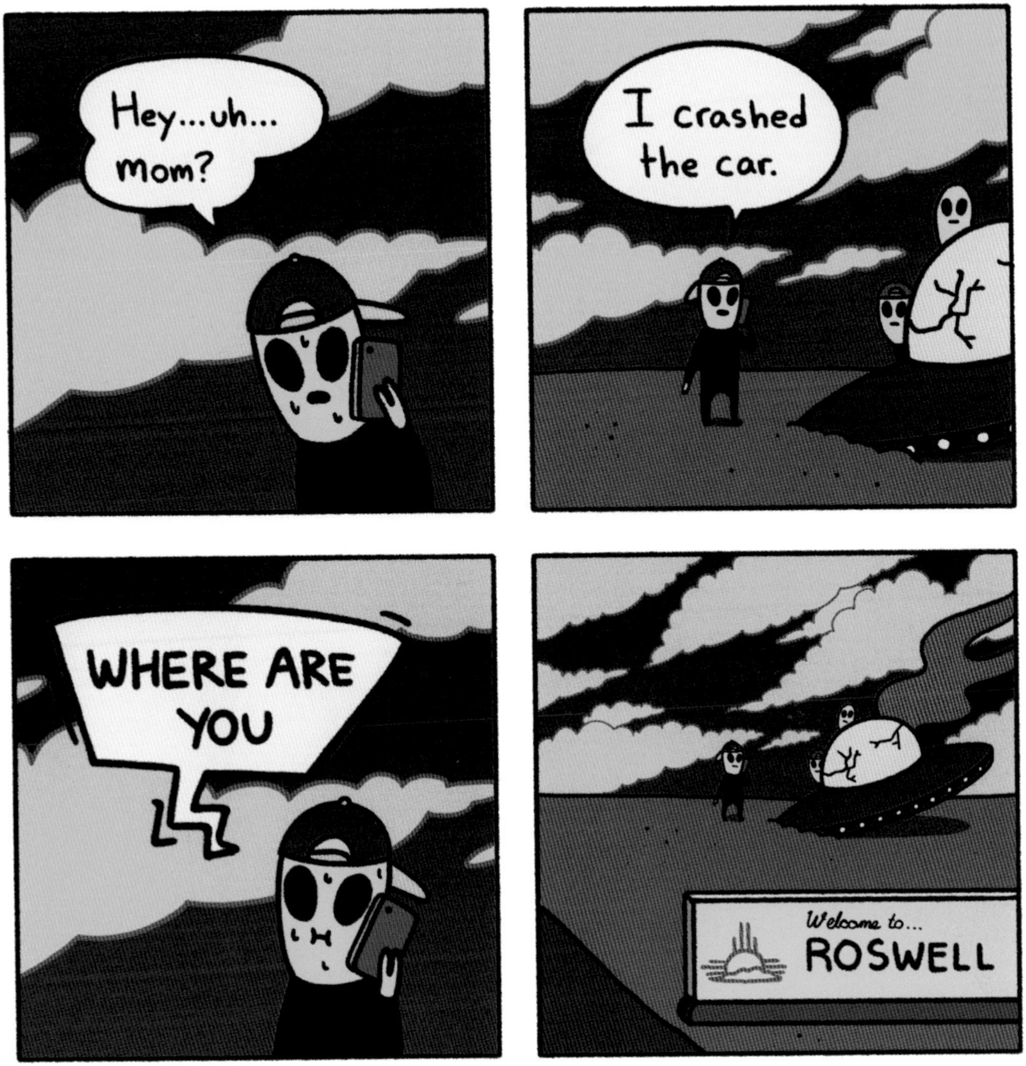
Hey...uh... mom?
I crashed the car.
WHERE ARE YOU
Welcome to...
ROSWELL

MAKING FRIENDS

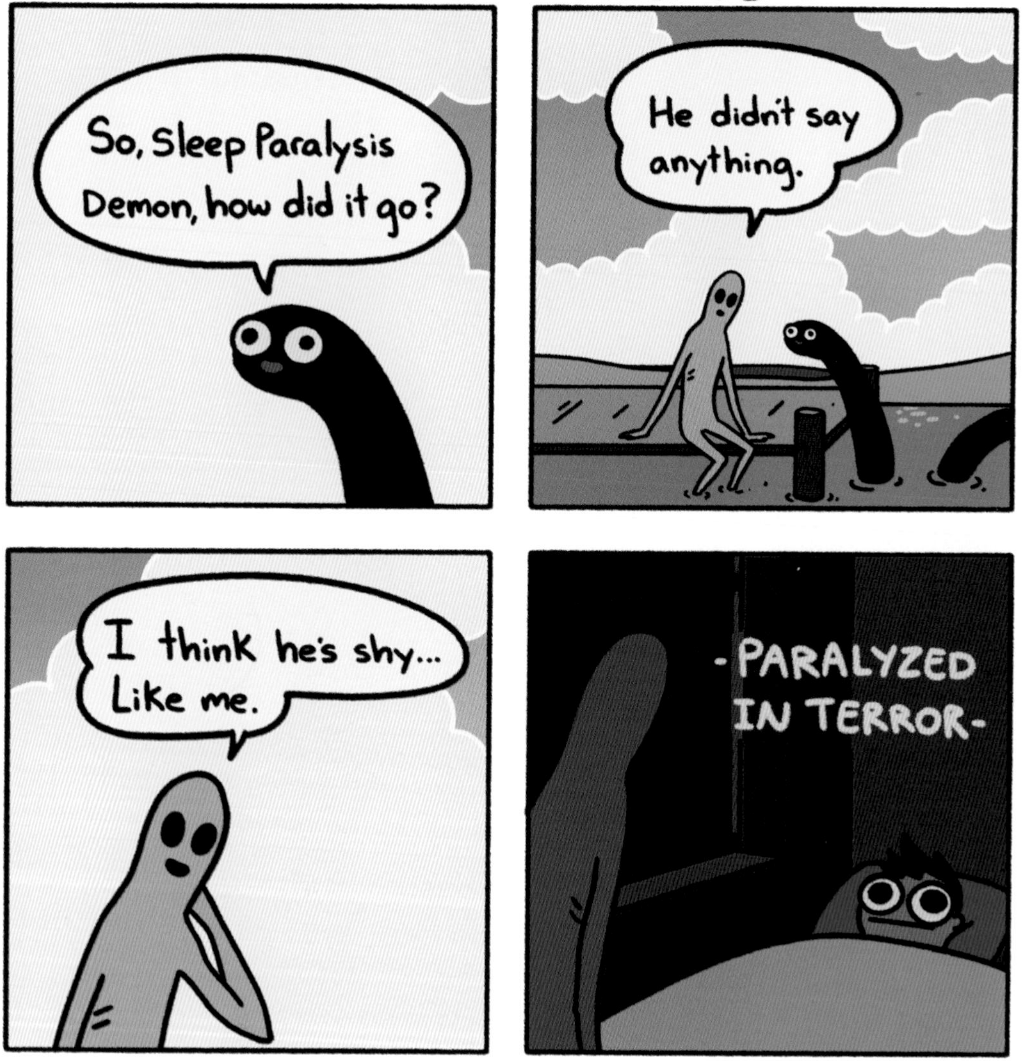
So, Sleep Paralysis Demon, how did it go?
He didn't say anything.
I think he's shy... Like me.
-PARALYZED IN TERROR-

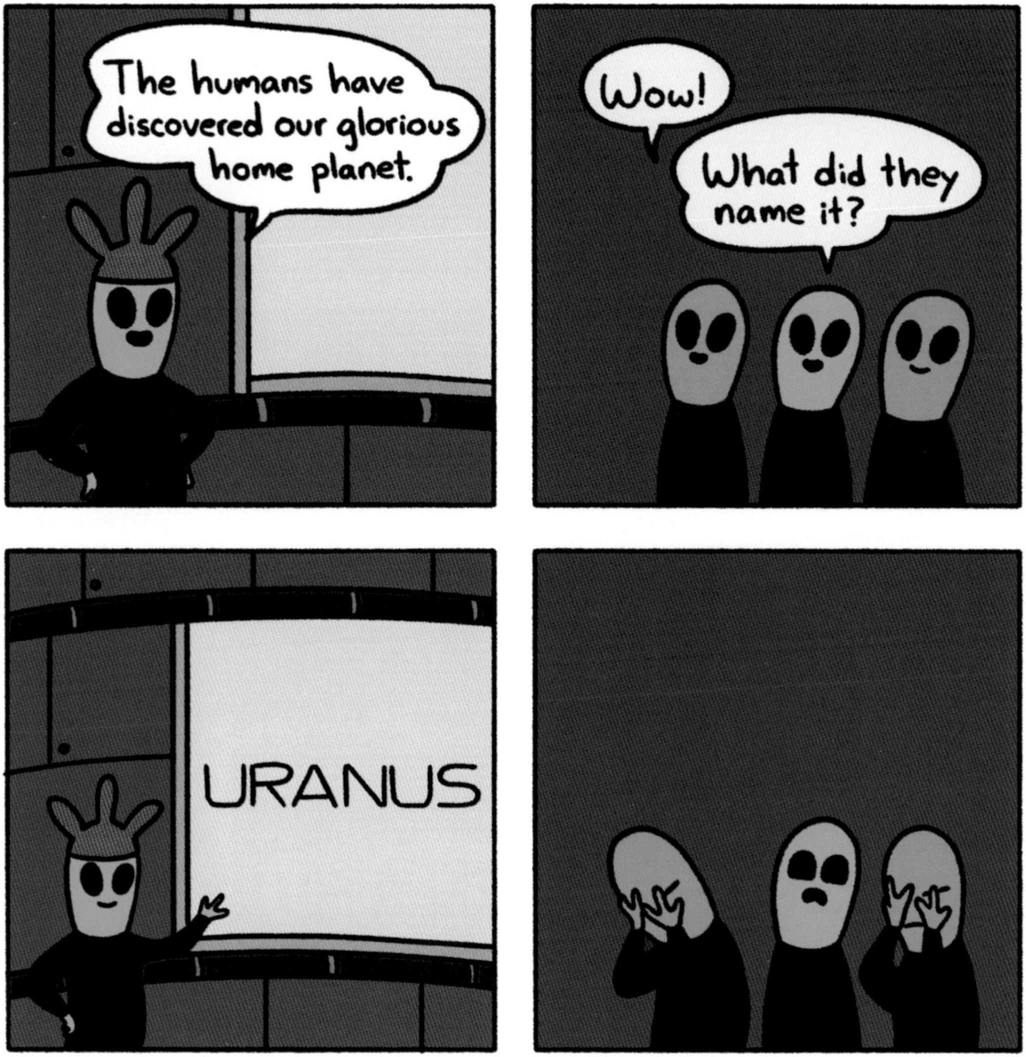

The humans have discovered our glorious home planet.
Wow!
What did they name it?
URANUS

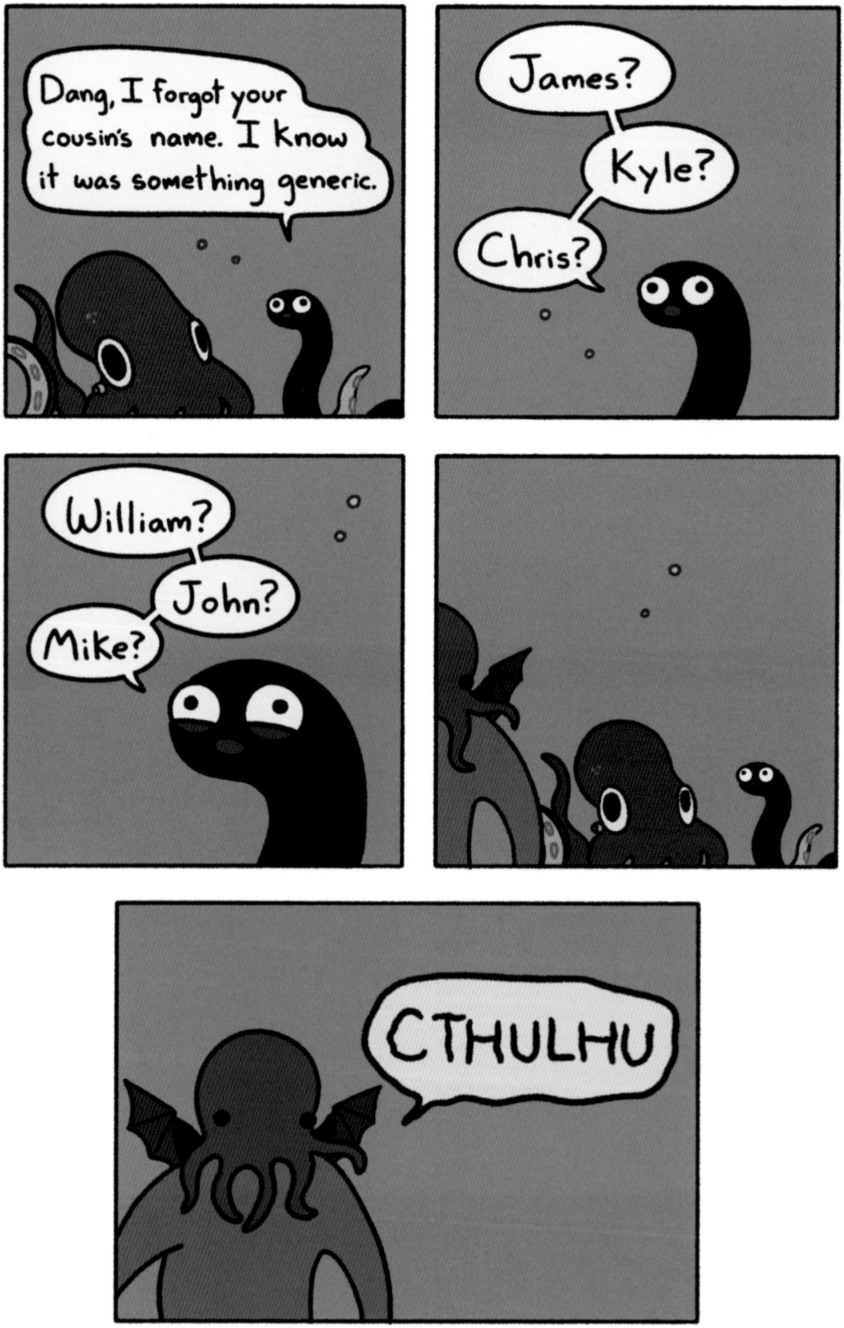
Dang, I forgot your cousin's name. I know it was something generic.
James?
Kyle?
Chris?
William?
John?
Mike?
CTHULHU

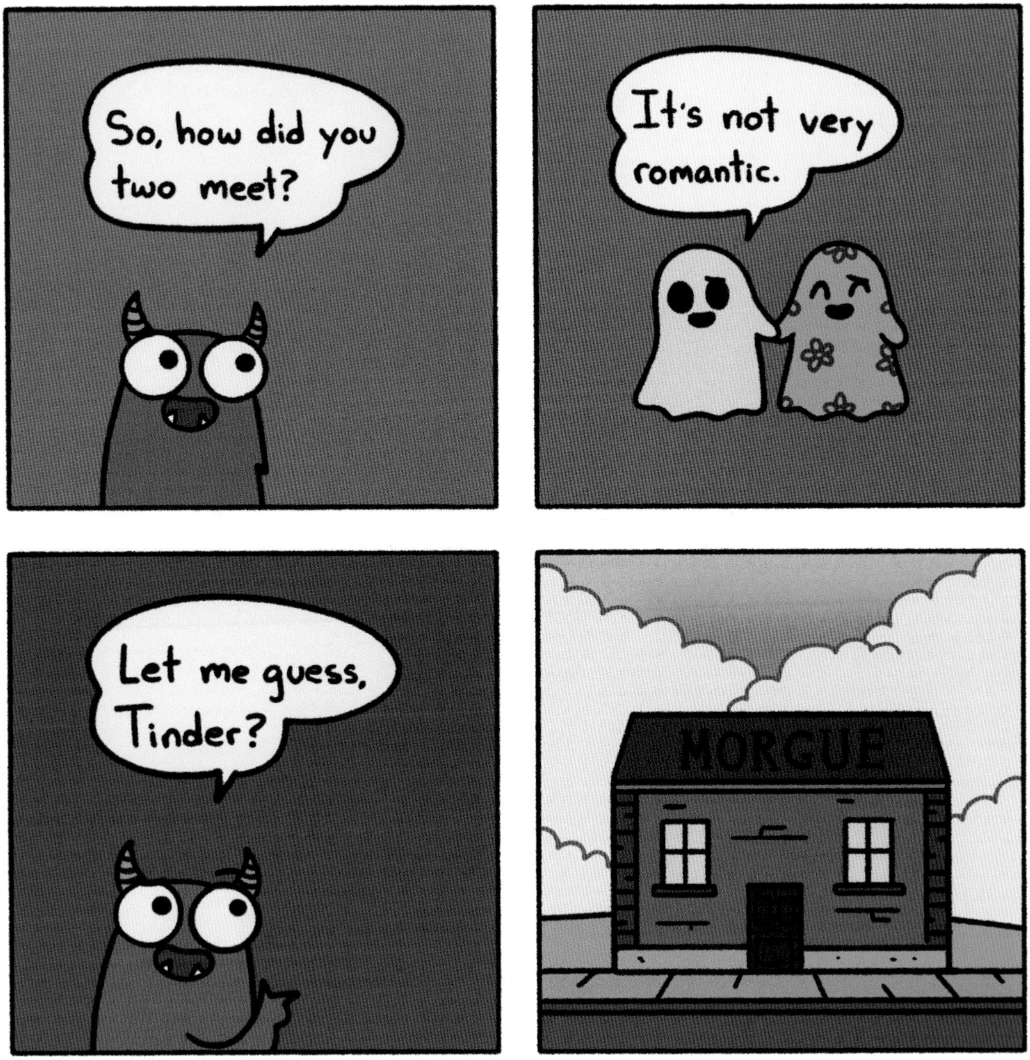
So, how did you two meet?
It's not very romantic.
Let me guess, Tinder?
MORGUE

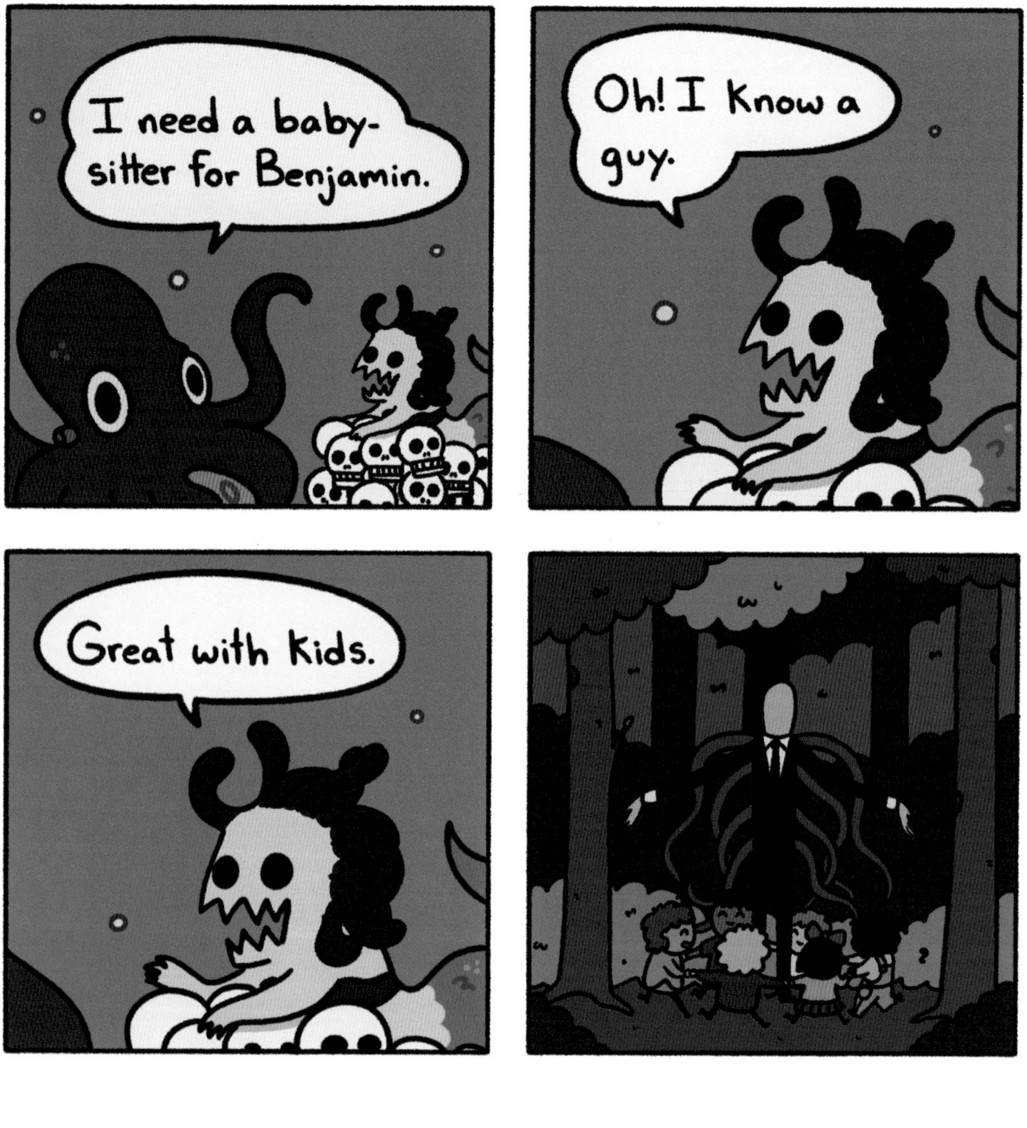
I need a baby-sitter for Benjamin.
Oh! I know a guy.
Great with kids.

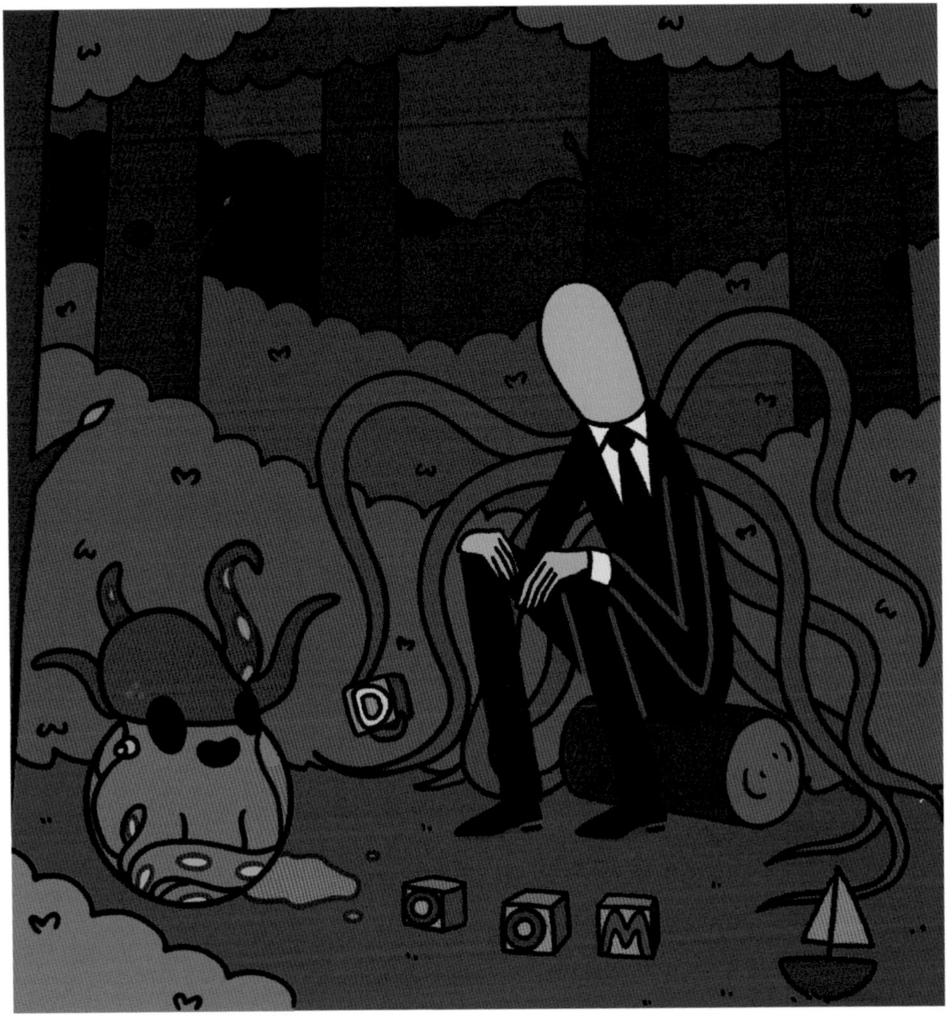
D
O
O
M

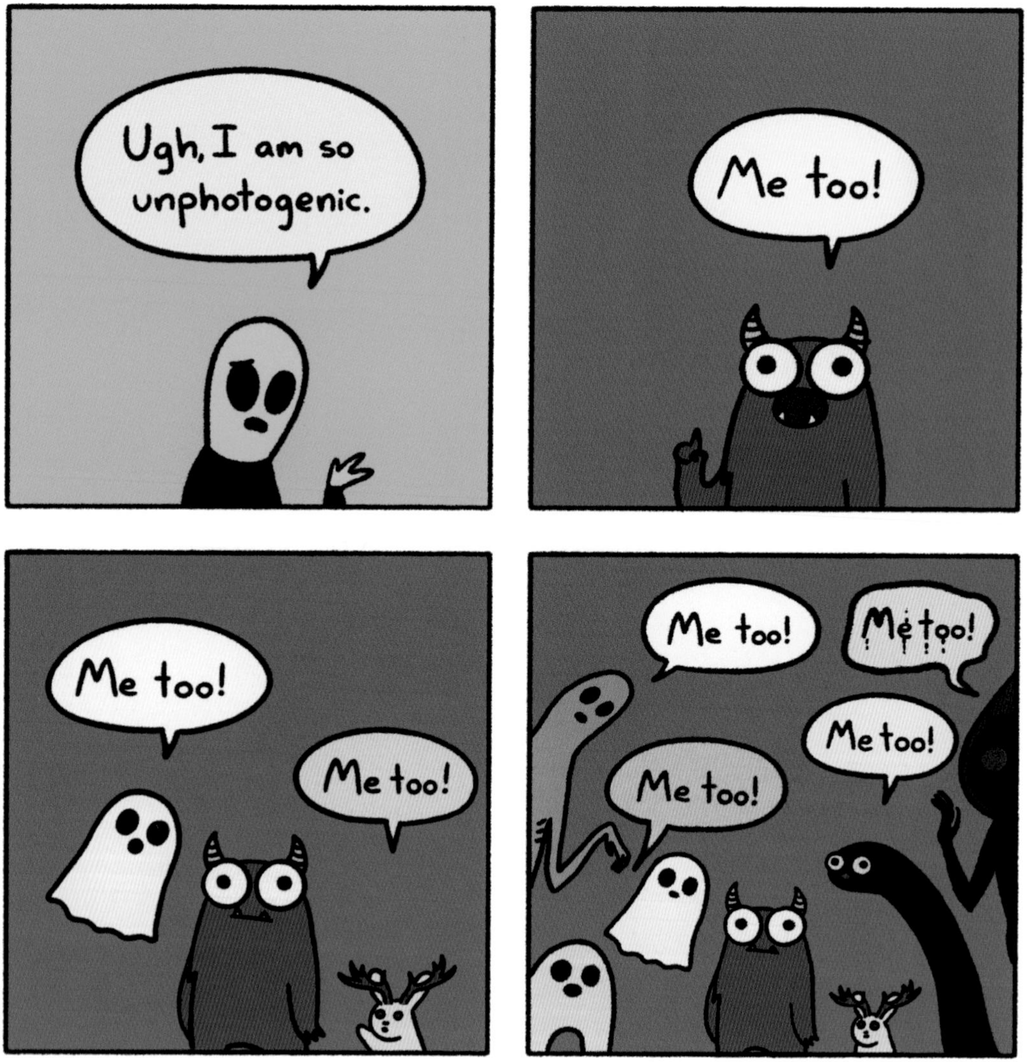
Ugh, I am so unphotogenic.
Me too!
Me too!
Me too!
Me too!
Me too!
Me too!
Me too!

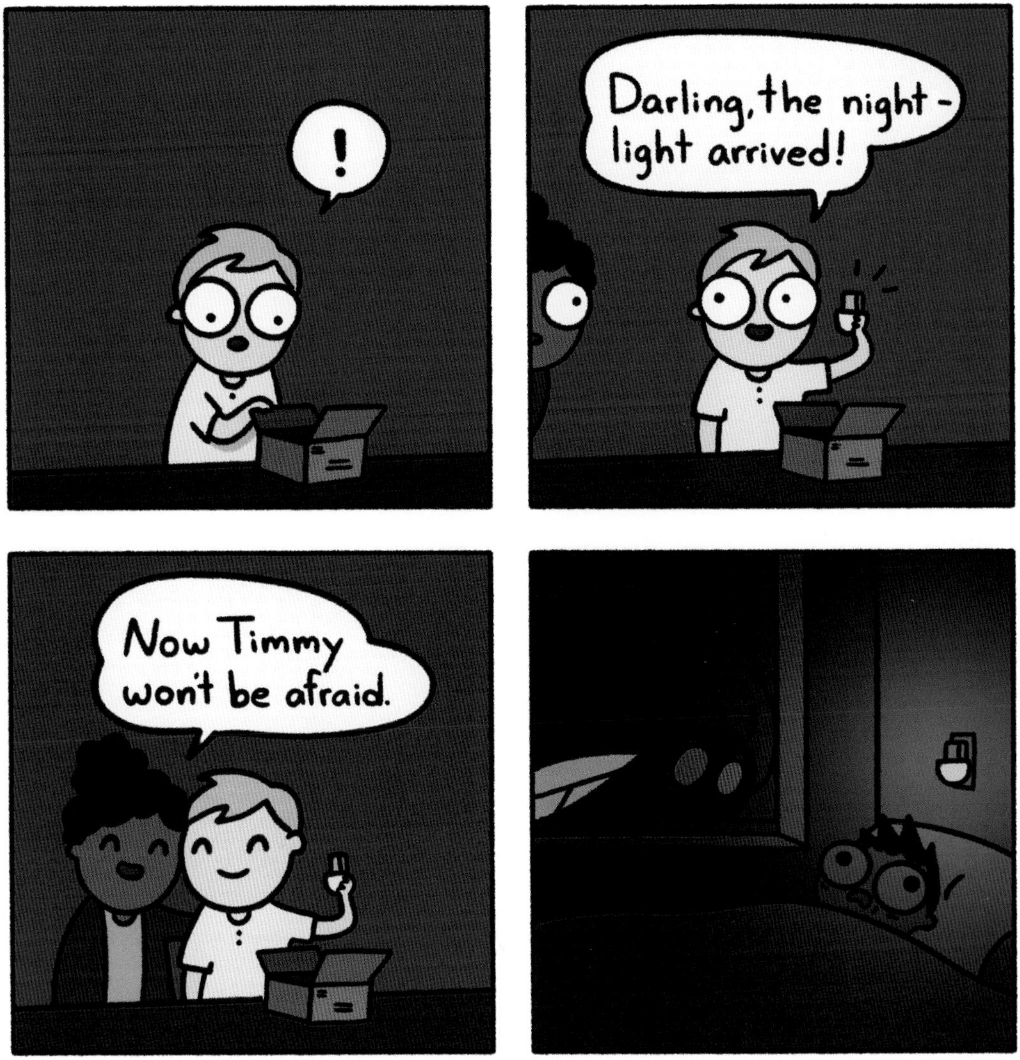
!
Darling, the night-light arrived!
Now Timmy won't be afraid.

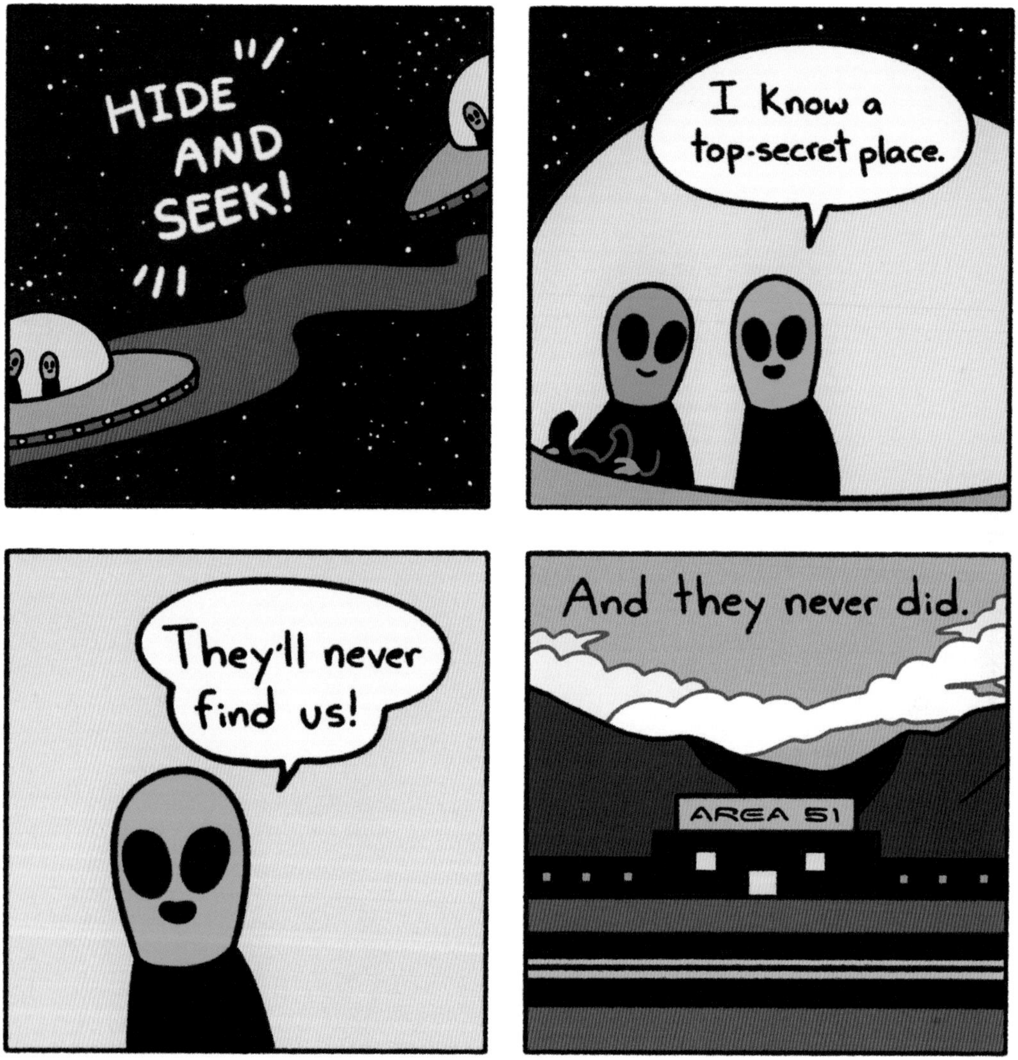
HIDE AND SEEK!
I Know a top-secret place.
They'll never find us!
And they never did.
AREA 51

GHOST PHOTOBOMB

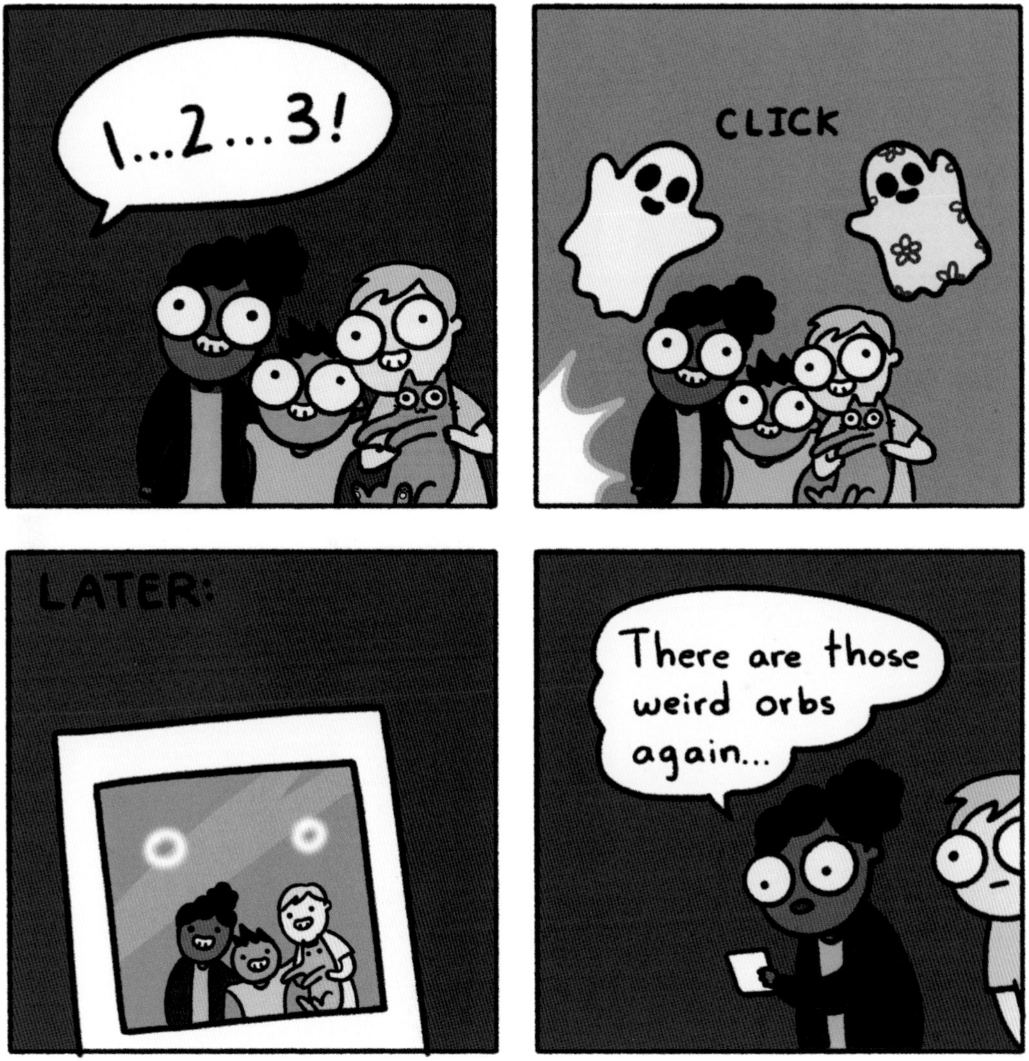
1...2...3!
CLICK
LATER:
There are those weird orbs again...

THE CALL OF CTHULHU

COME ON, CTHULHU. PICK UP THE PHONE. YOUR ANXIETY DOES NOT CONTROL YOU.
YOU CAN DO IT.

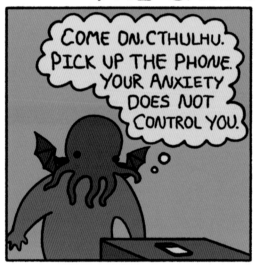

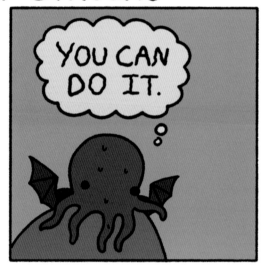

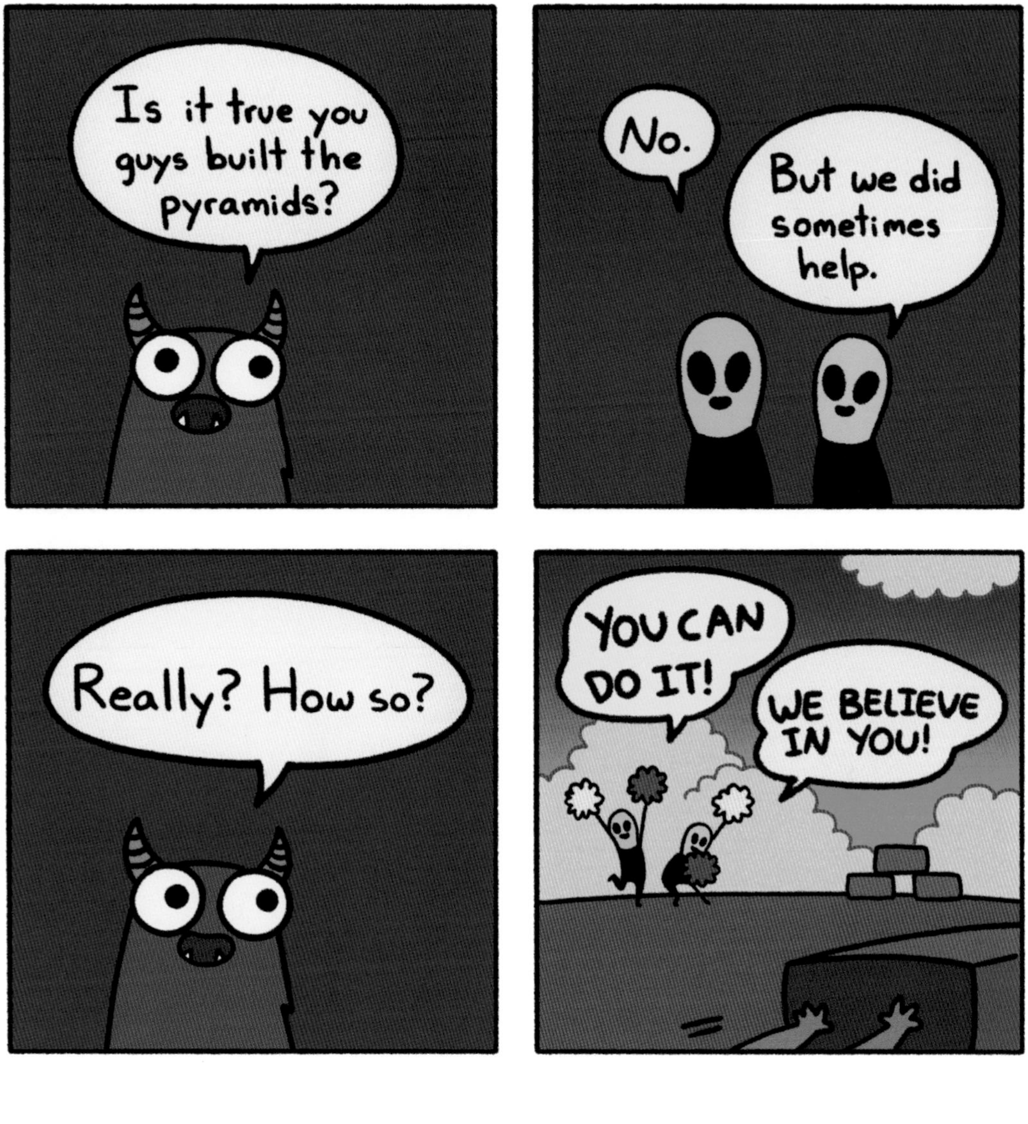

Is it true you guys built the pyramids?
No.
But we did sometimes help.
Really? How so?
YOU CAN DO IT!
WE BELIEVE IN YOU!

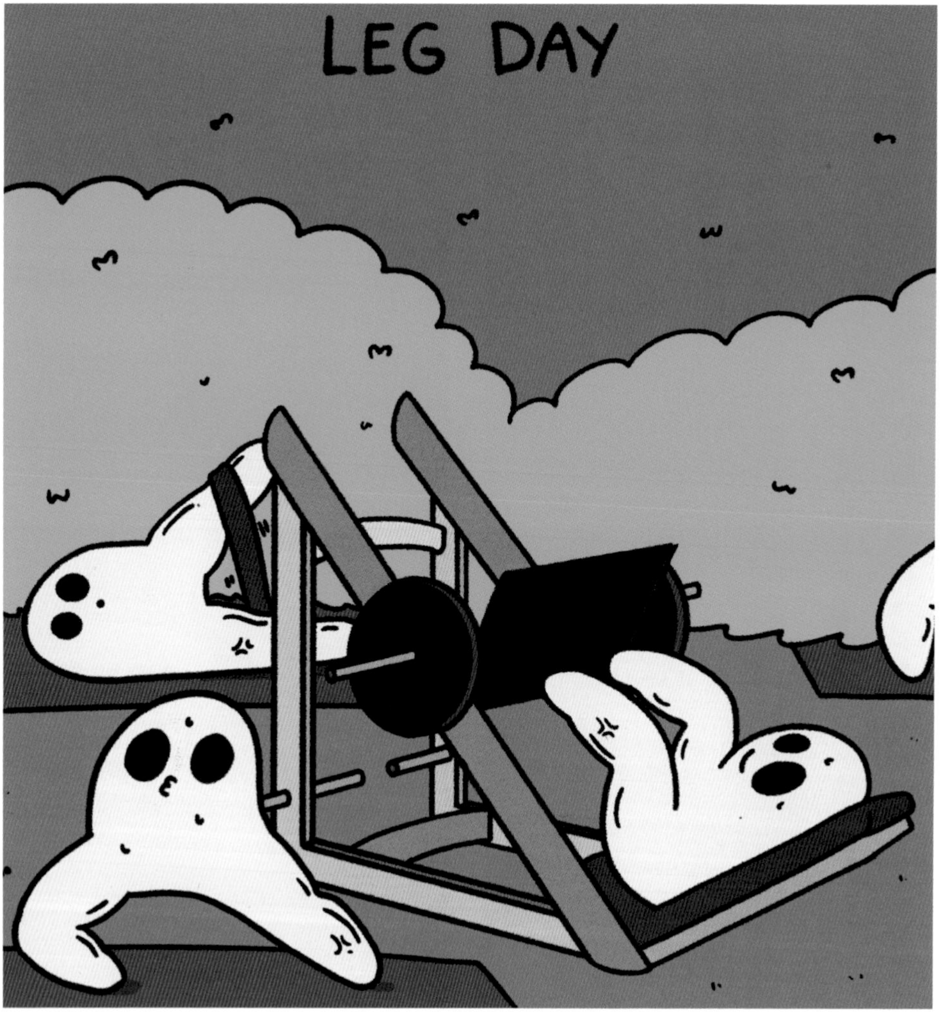
LEG DAY

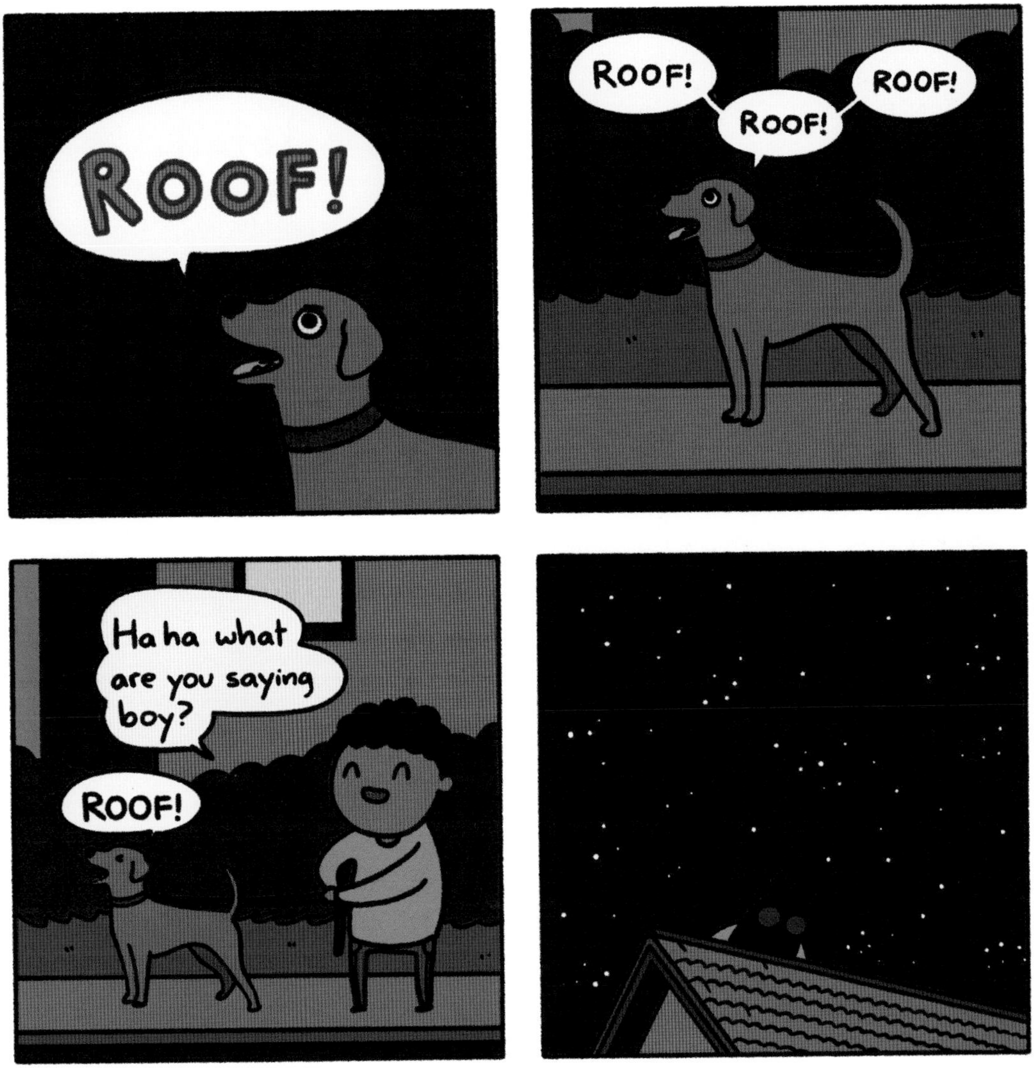
ROOF!
ROOF!
ROOF!
ROOF!
Ha ha what are you saying boy?
ROOF!

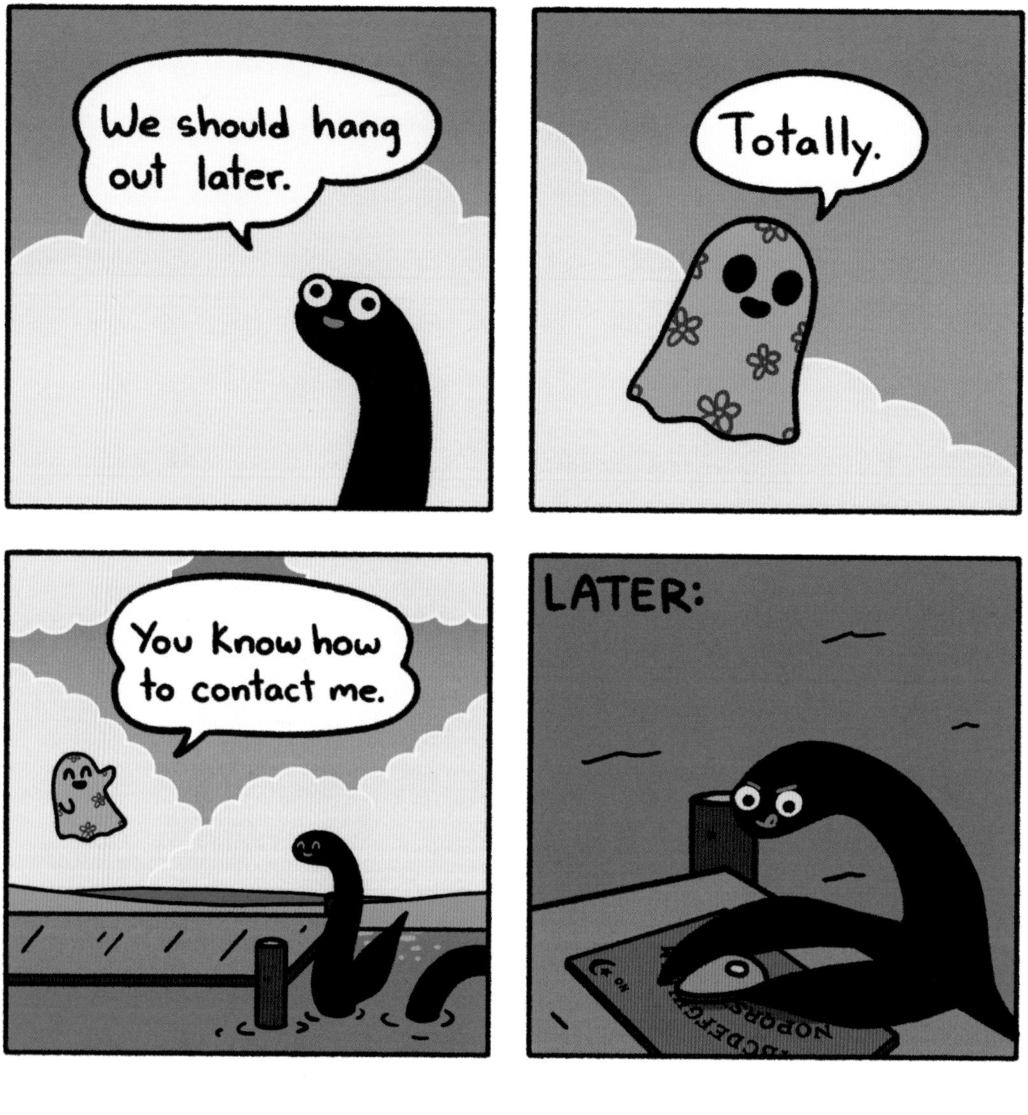
We should hang out later.
Totally.
You know how to contact me.
LATER:

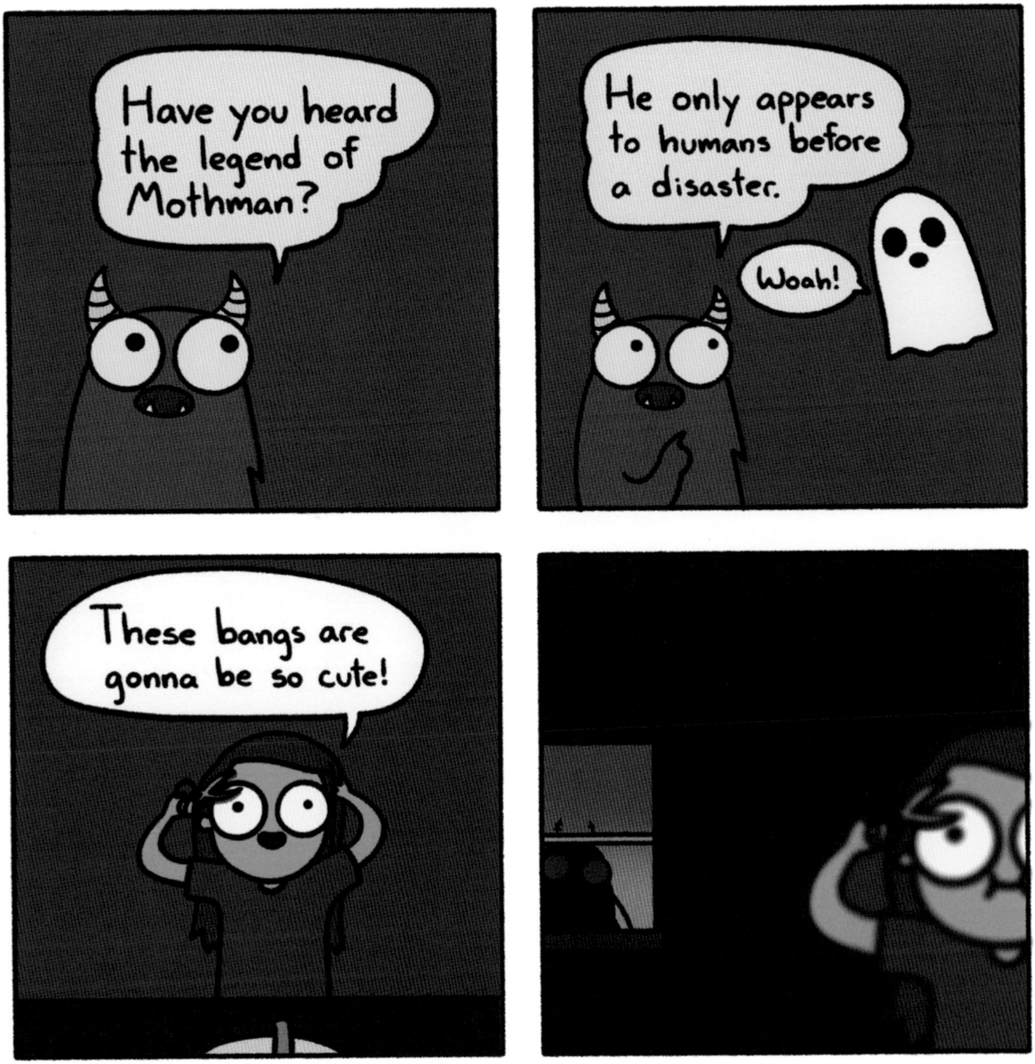
Have you heard the legend of Mothman?
He only appears to humans before a disaster.
Woah!
These bangs are gonna be so cute!

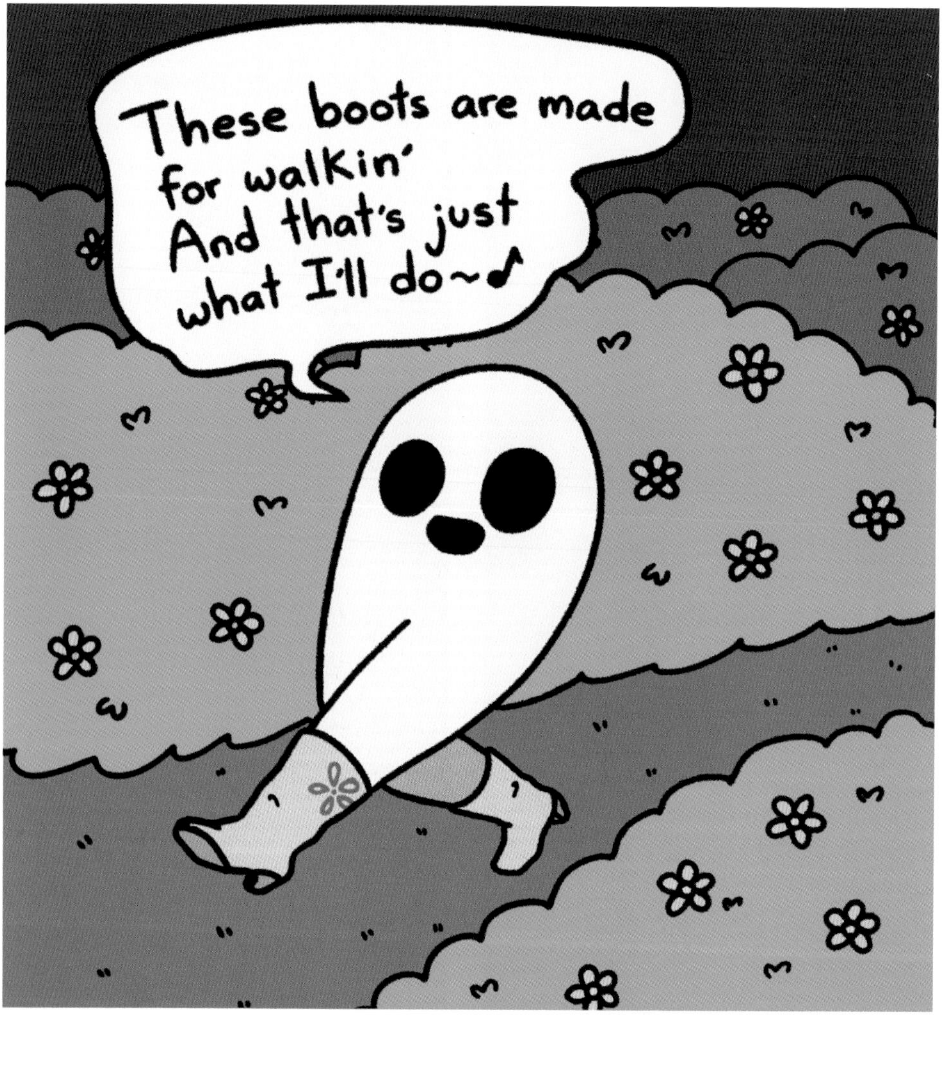
These boots are made for walkin'
And that's just what I'll do~♪

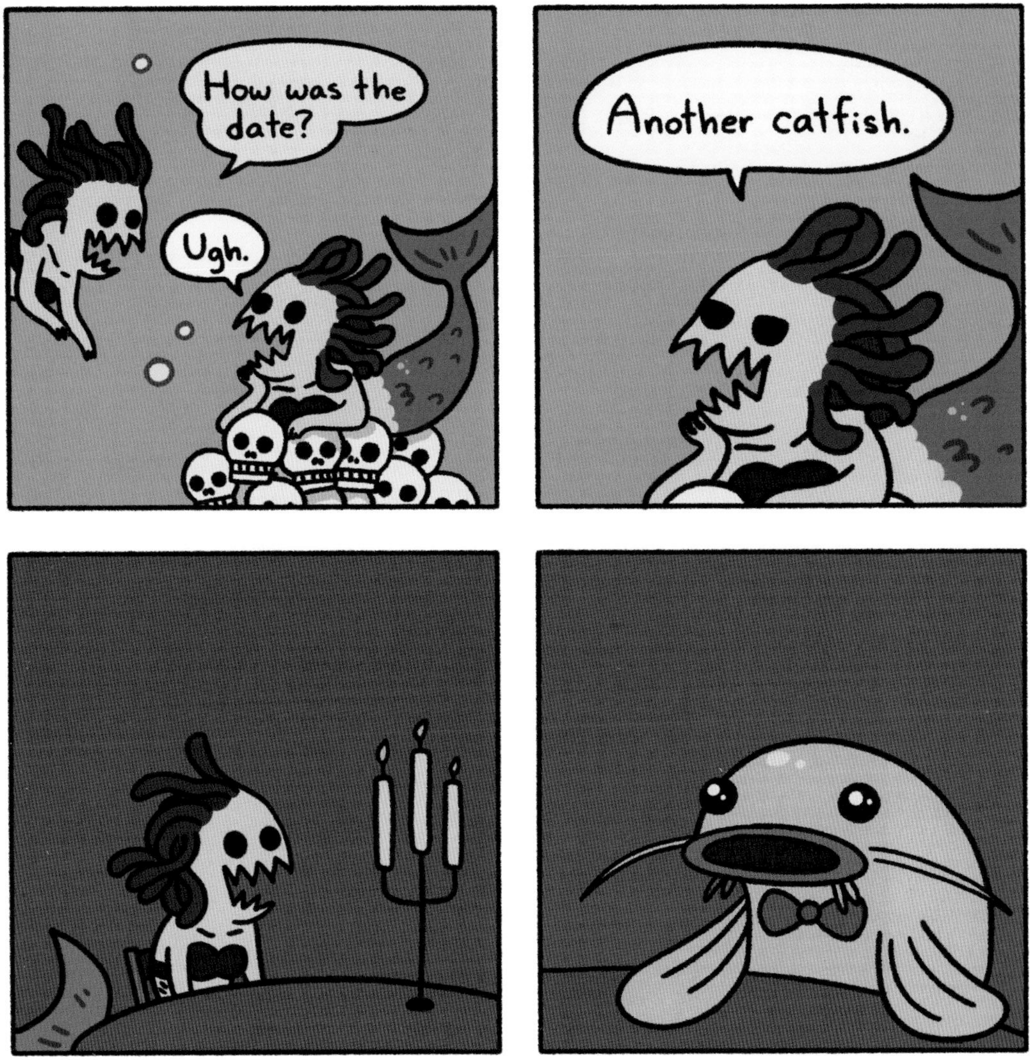
How was the date?
Ugh.
Another catfish.

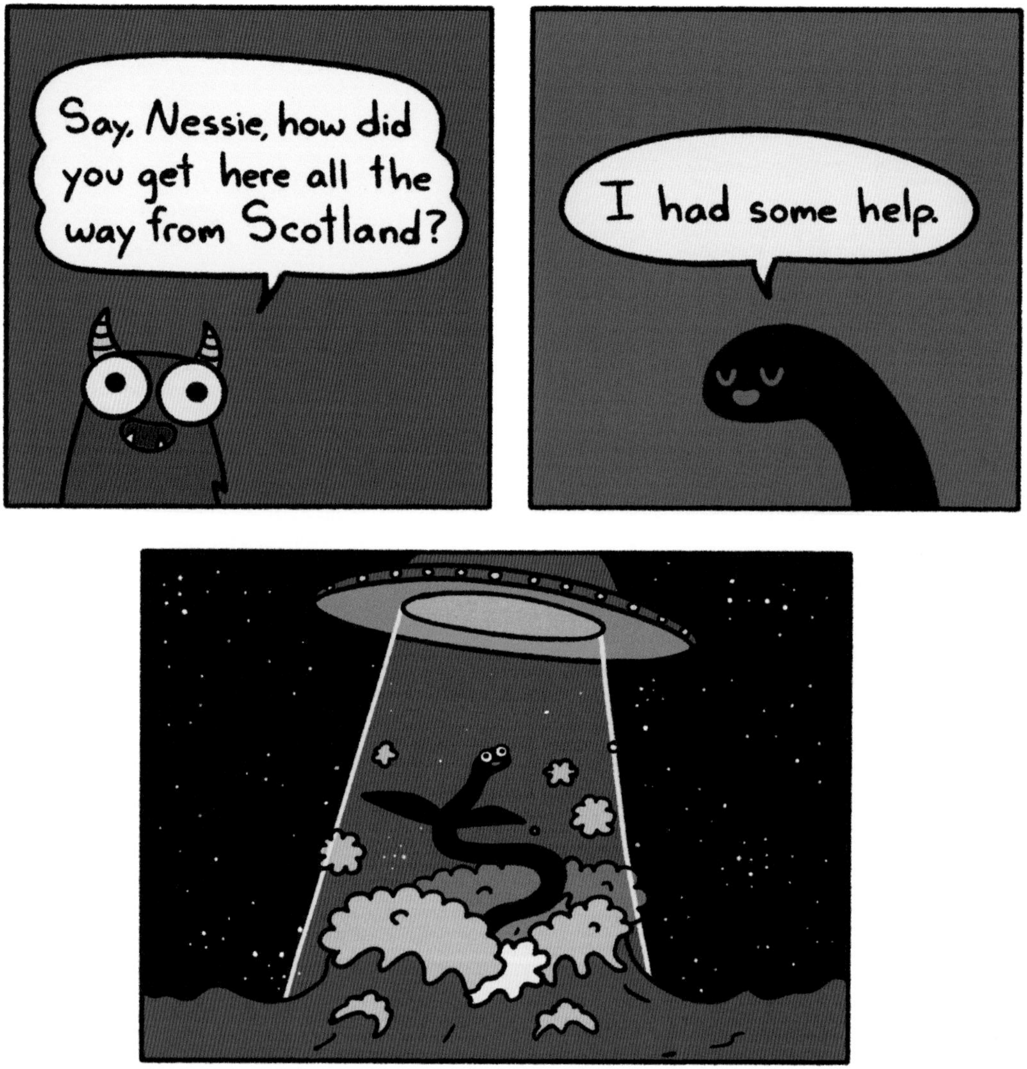
Say, Nessie, how did you get here all the way from Scotland?
I had some help.

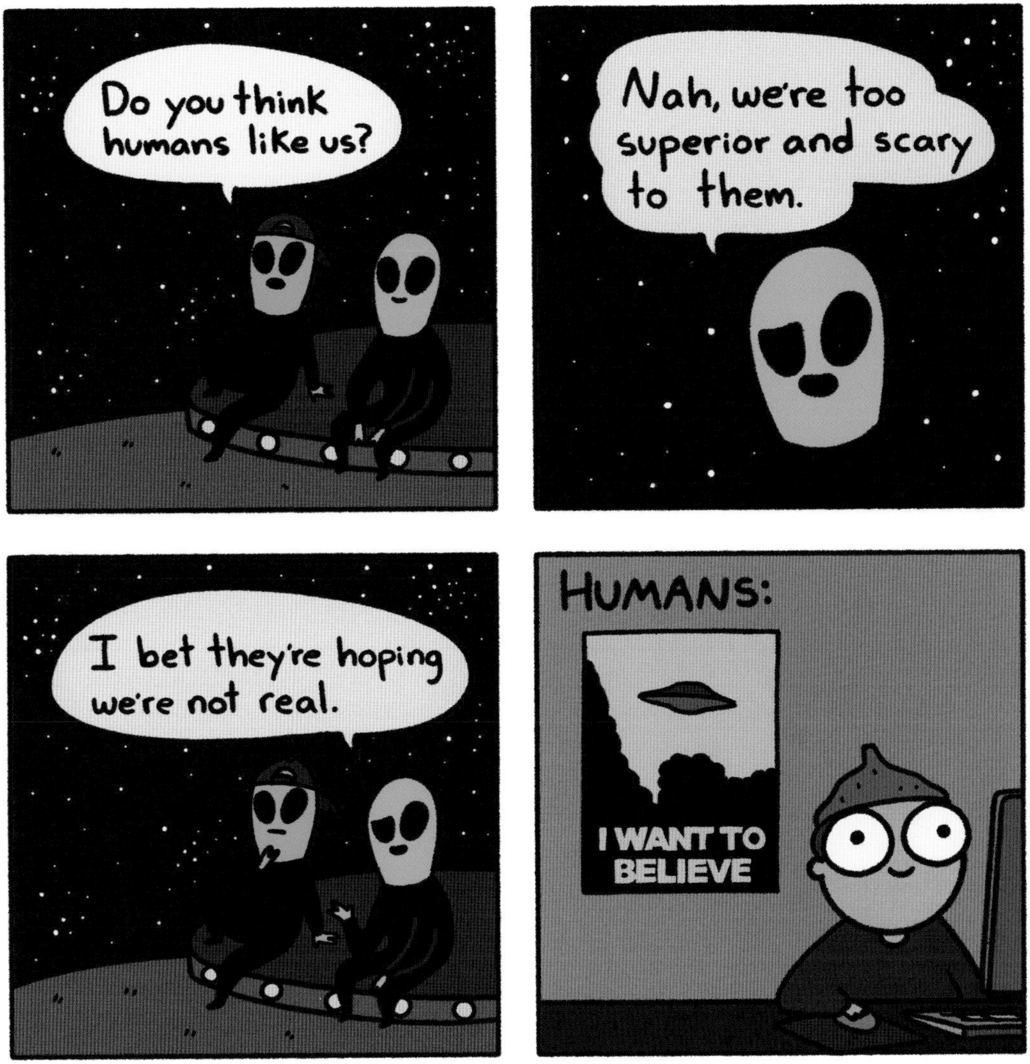
Do you think humans like us?
Nah, we're too superior and scary to them.
I bet they're hoping we're not real.
HUMANS:
I WANT TO BELIEVE

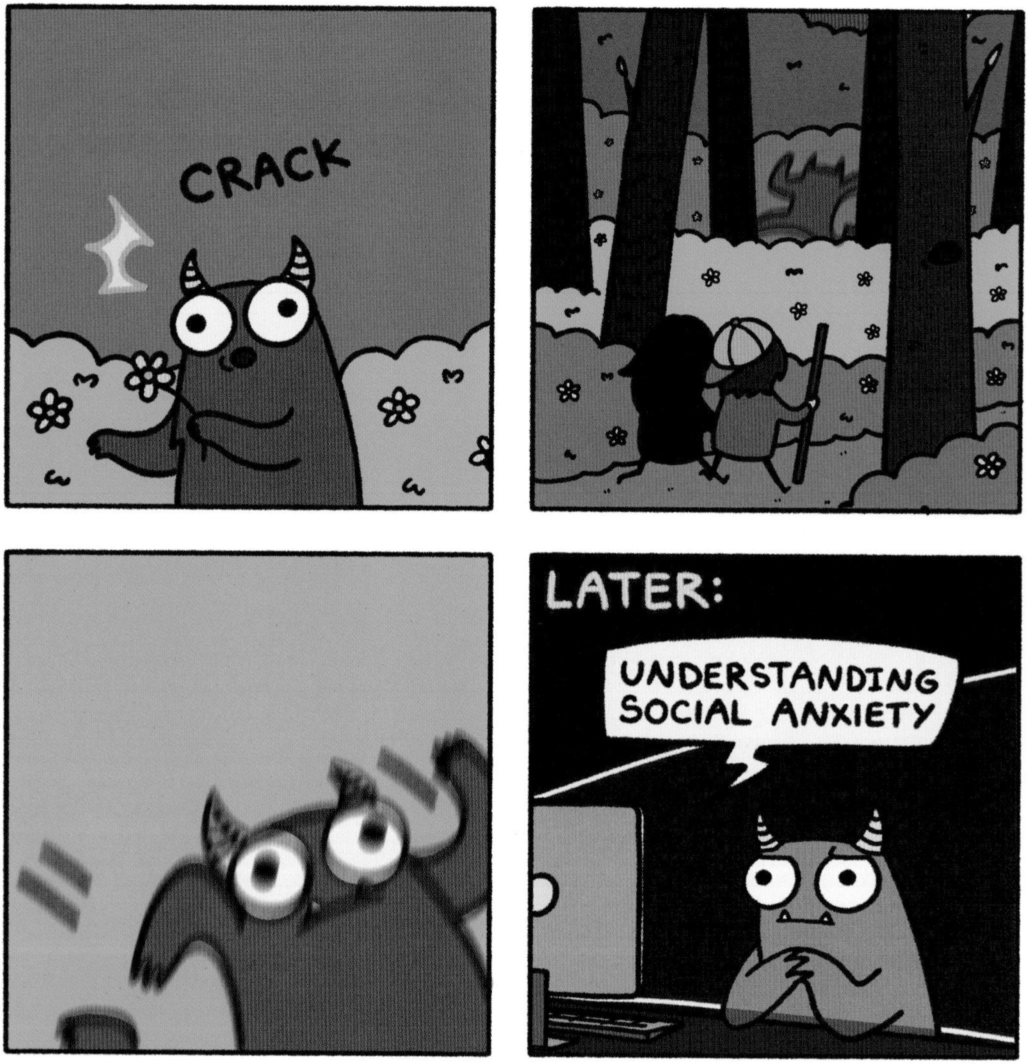
CRACK
LATER:
UNDERSTANDING SOCIAL ANXIETY

THE CALL OF CTHULHU PT. 2

RING
TAKE ME BACK, MARIE.

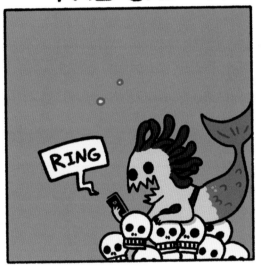

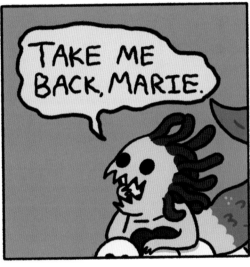

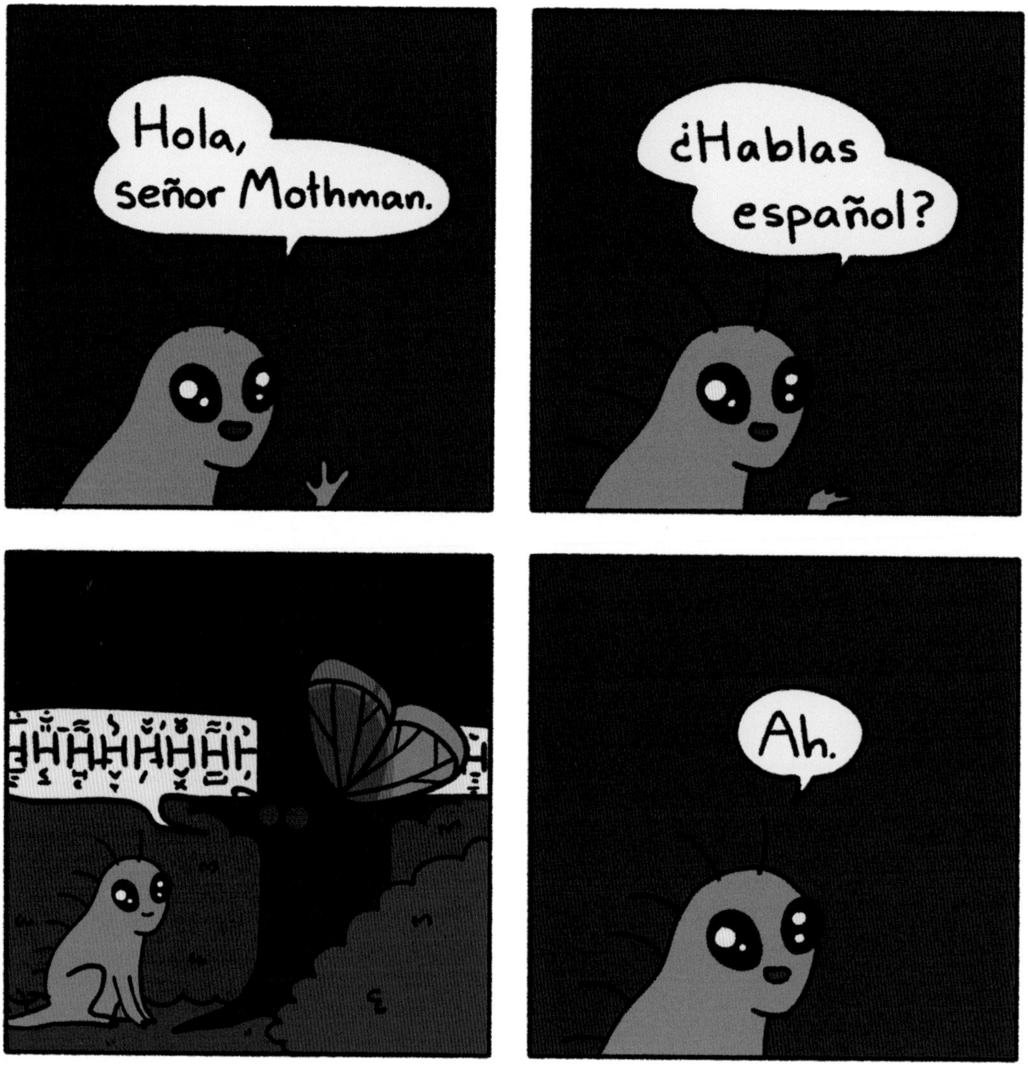
Hola, señor Mothman.
¿Hablas español?
Ah.

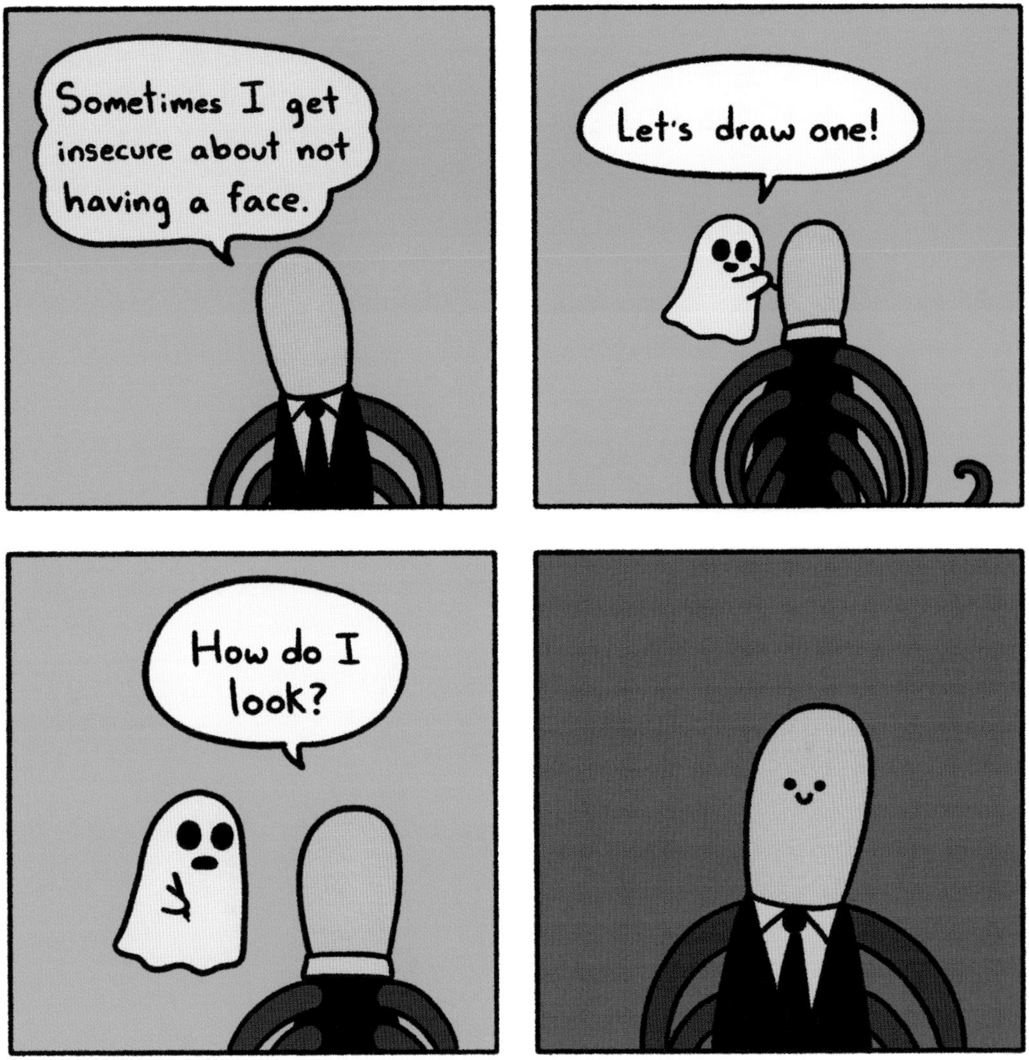
Sometimes I get insecure about not having a face.
Let's draw one!
How do I look?

LEARNING EACH OTHER'S LANGUAGES

Cryptid.
Criptido.
Siren.
Sirena.
Extraterrestrial.
Extraterrestre.
Chuppie. I think we're gonna nail this.

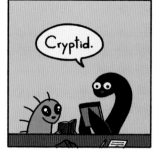

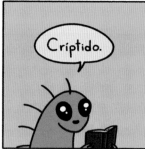

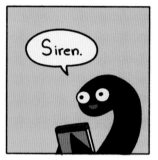

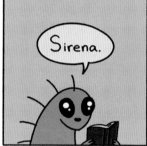

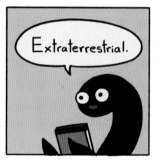

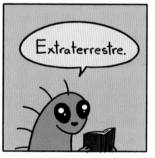

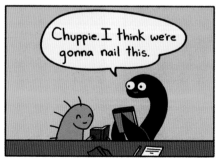

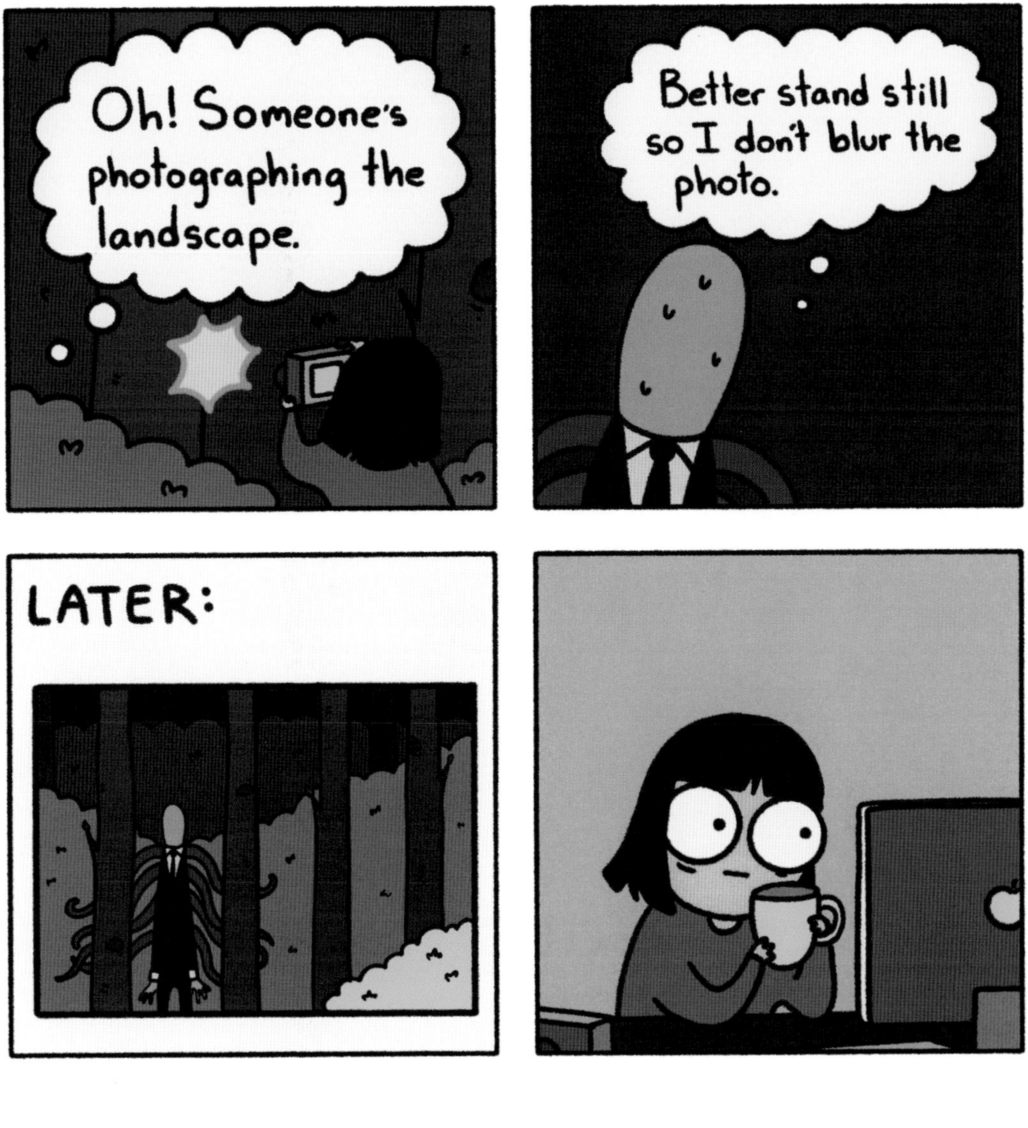
Oh! Someone's photographing the landscape.
Better stand still so I don't blur the photo.
LATER:

Yeah... High-waisted jeans don't work for me.

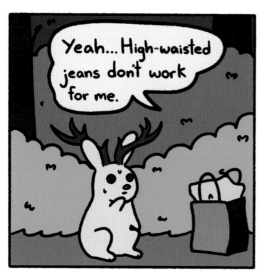

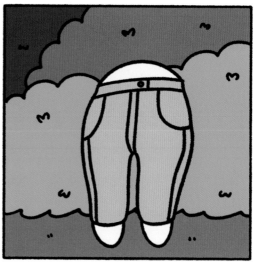

NOT LIKE OTHER GIRLS

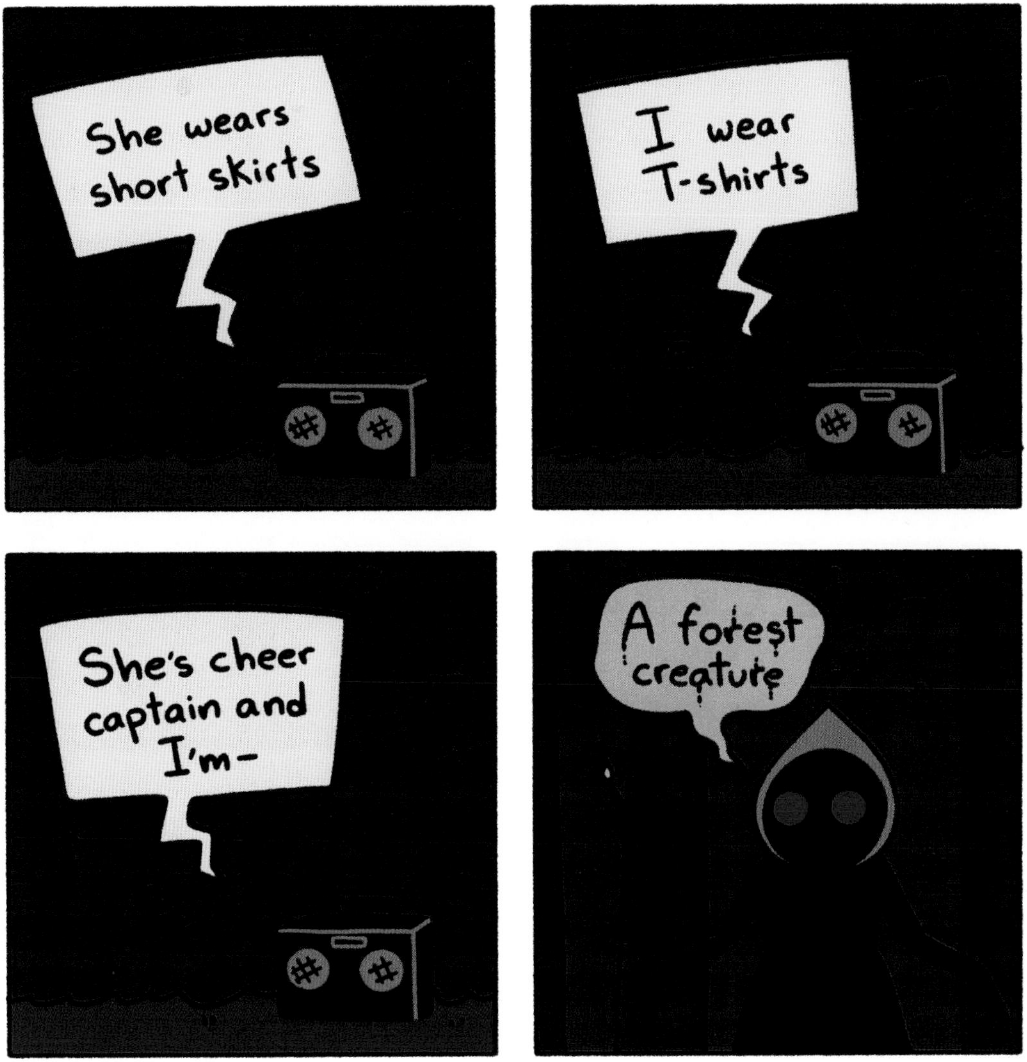

She wears short skirts
I wear T-shirts
She's cheer captain and I'm-
A forest creature

Good night, darling.
I hope you haunt my dreams.

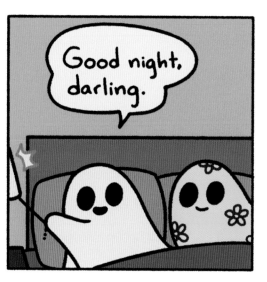

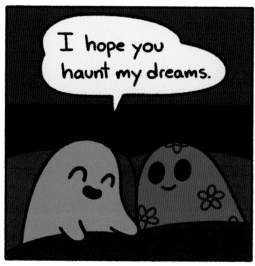

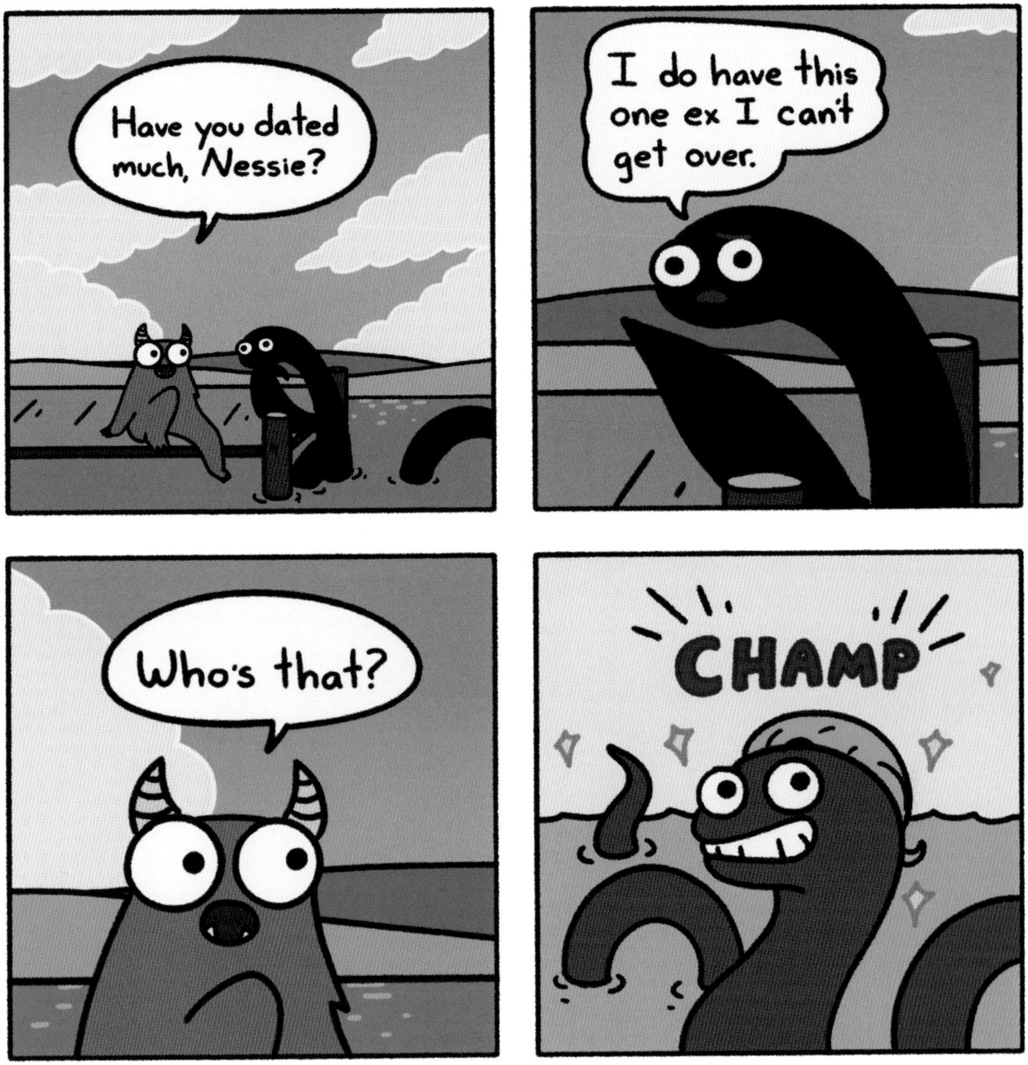
Have you dated much, Nessie?
I do have this one ex I can't get over.
Who's that?
CHAMP

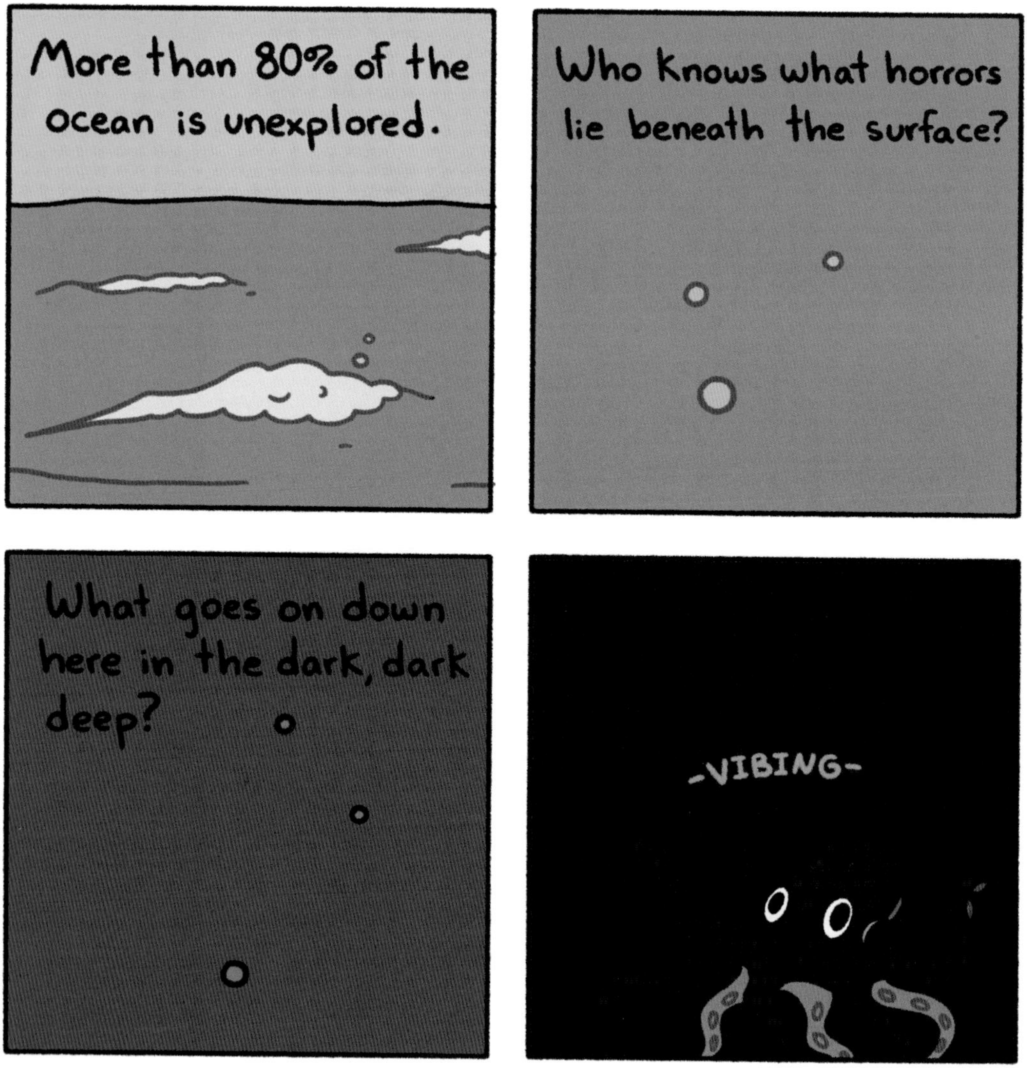
More than 80% of the ocean is unexplored.
Who knows what horrors lie beneath the surface?
What goes on down here in the dark, dark deep?
-VIBING-

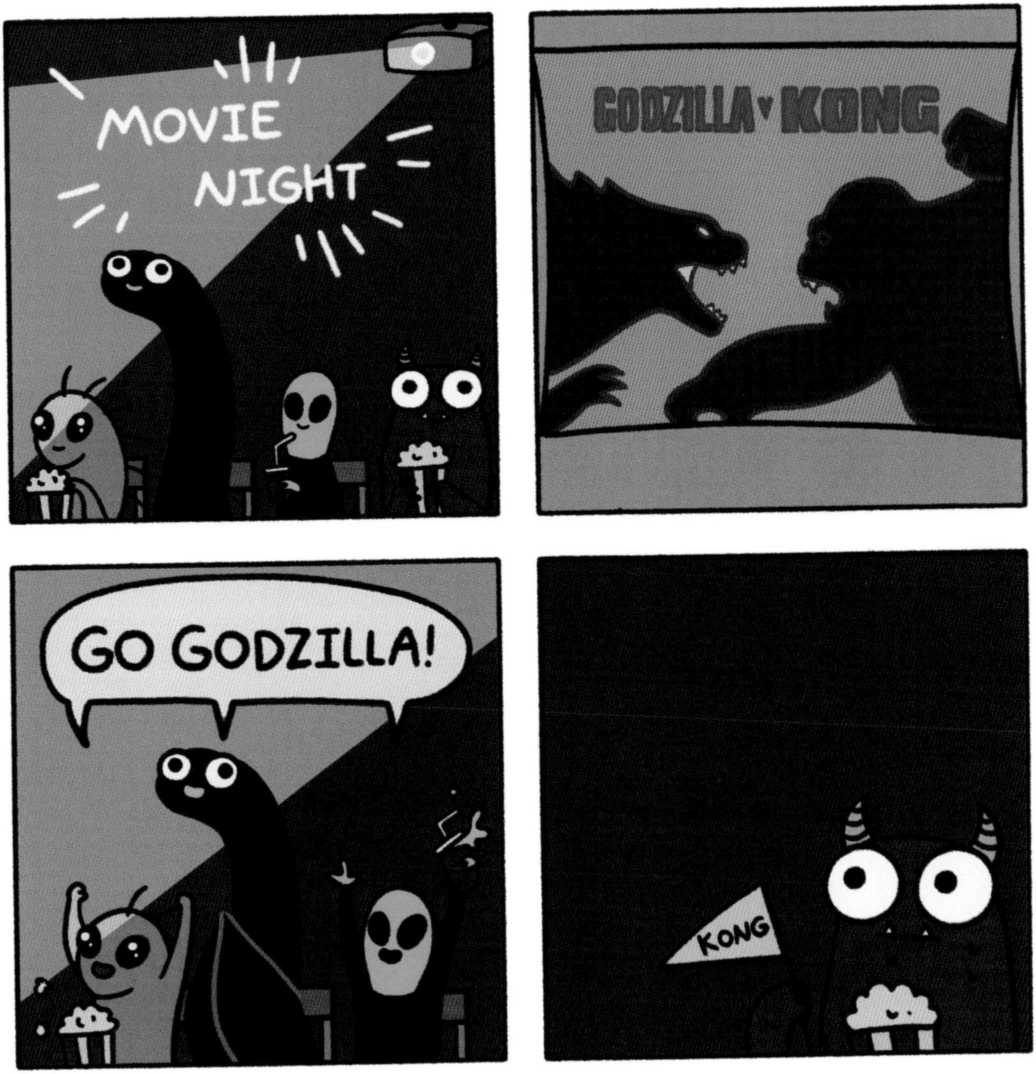
MOVIE NIGHT
GODZILLA v KONG
GO GODZILLA!
KONG

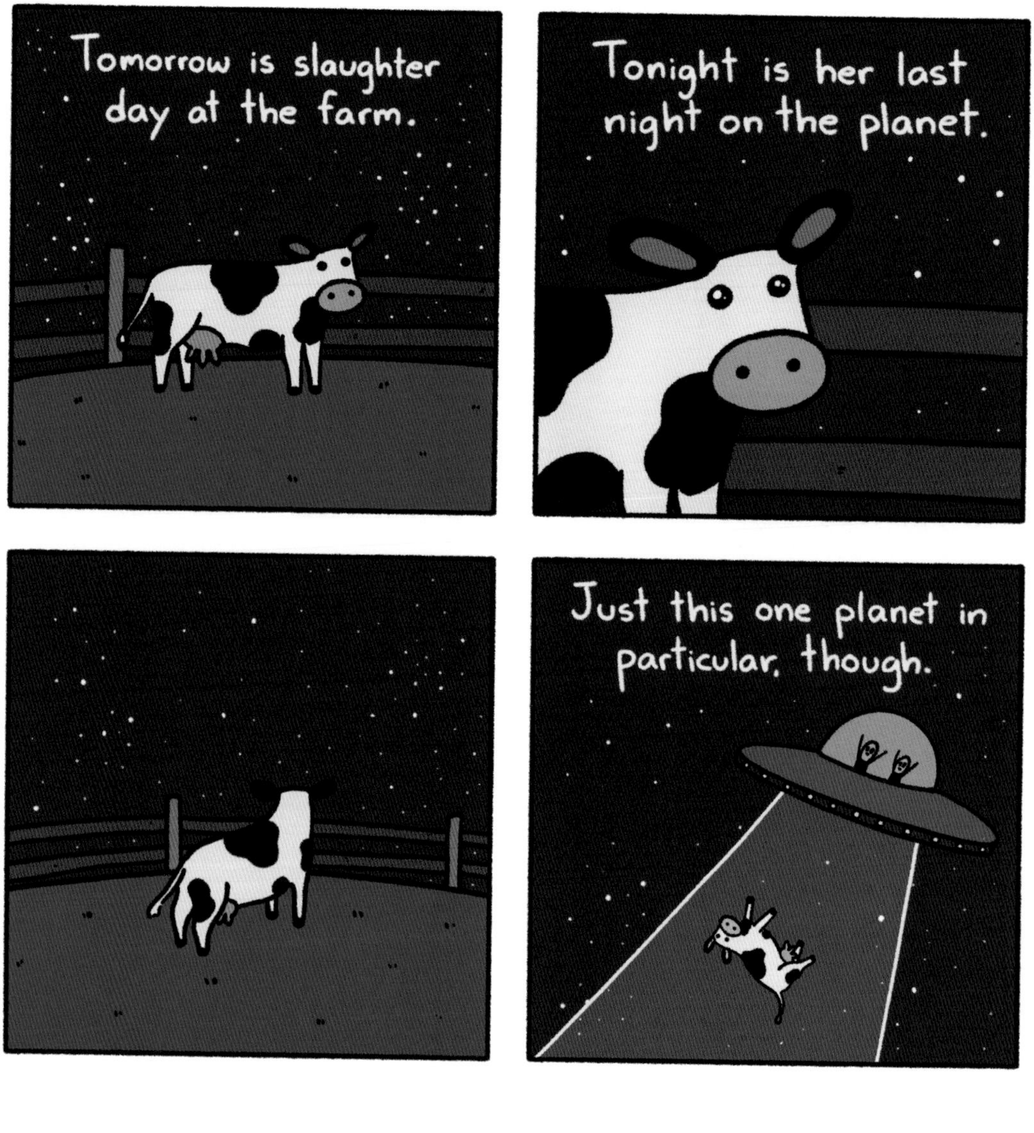
Tomorrow is slaughter day at the farm.
Tonight is her last night on the planet.
Just this one planet in particular, though.

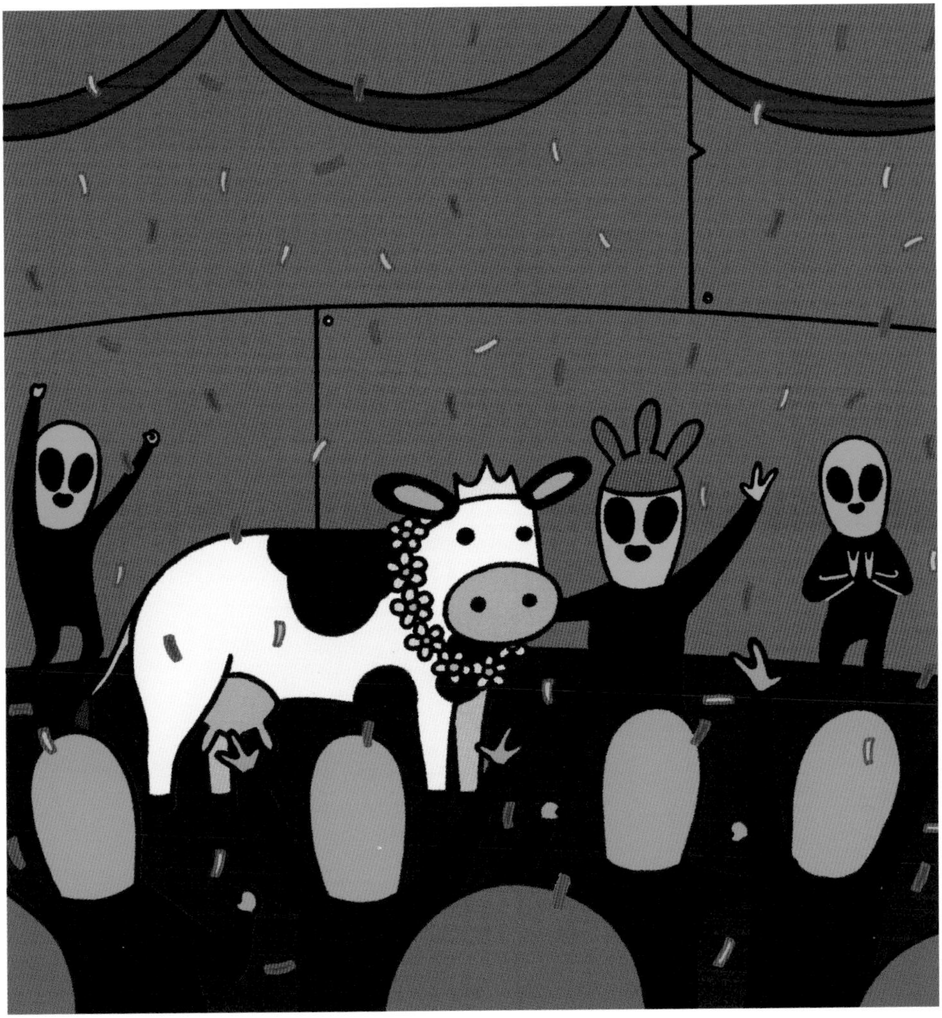

I have no luck on dating apps. Everyone ghosts.
What did you expect on a Cryptid dating app, Sam.

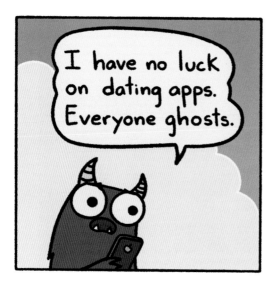

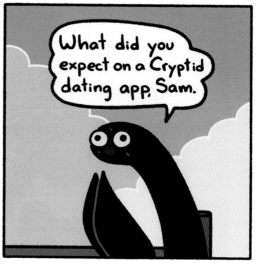

ROLE MODEL

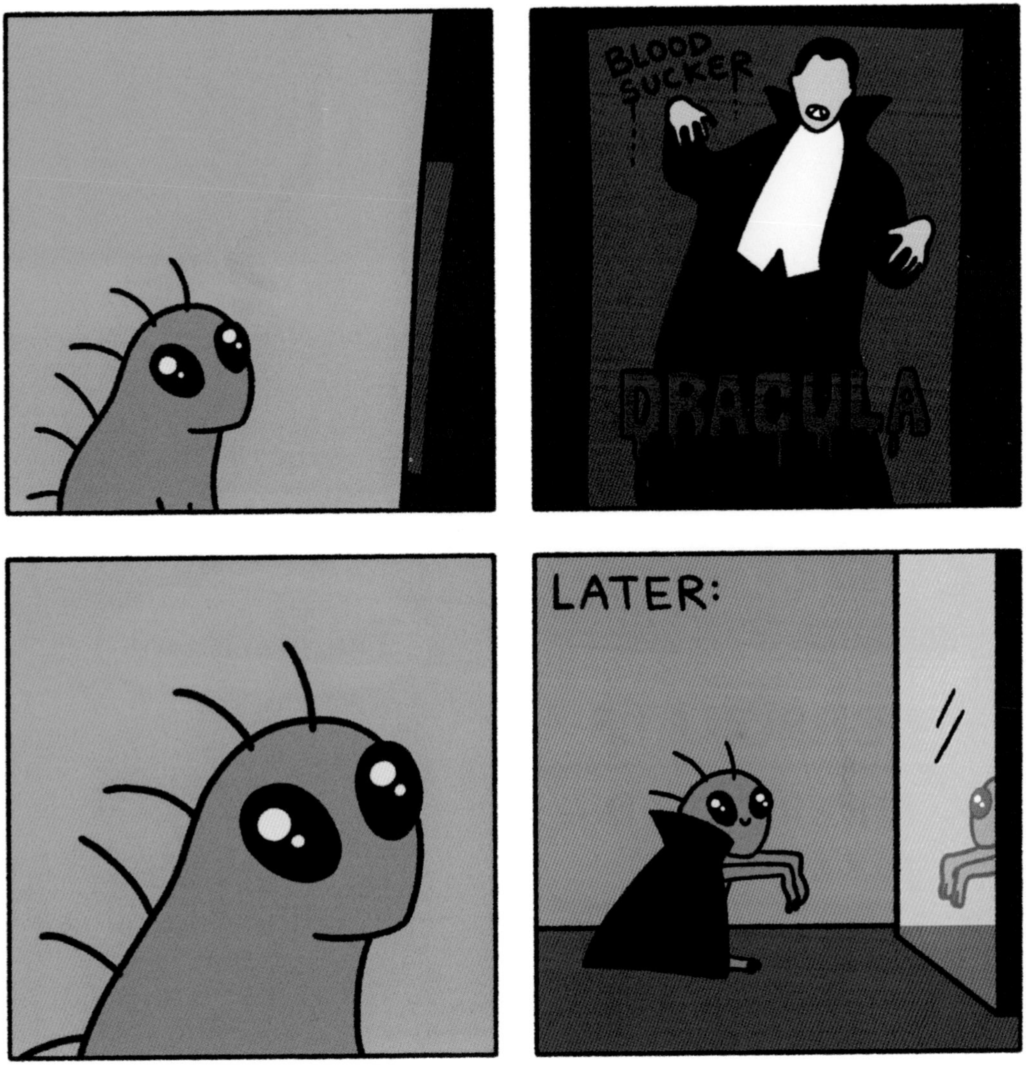
BLOOD SUCKER
DRACULA
LATER:

EARLIER:

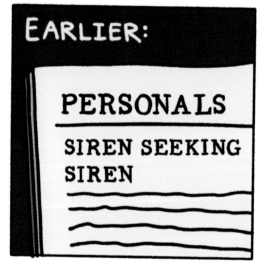

PERSONALS

SIREN SEEKING
SIREN

This is awkward.

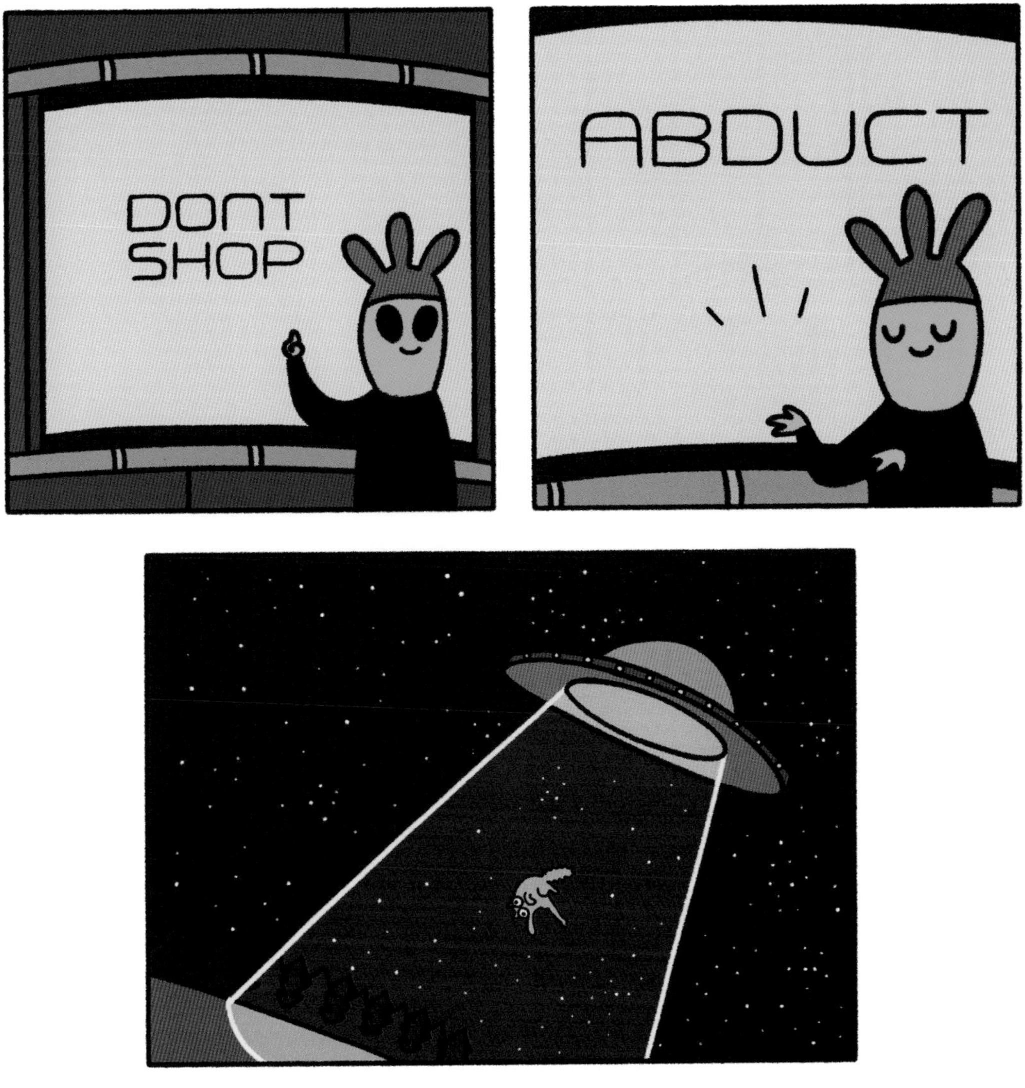
DONT
SHOP
ABDUCT

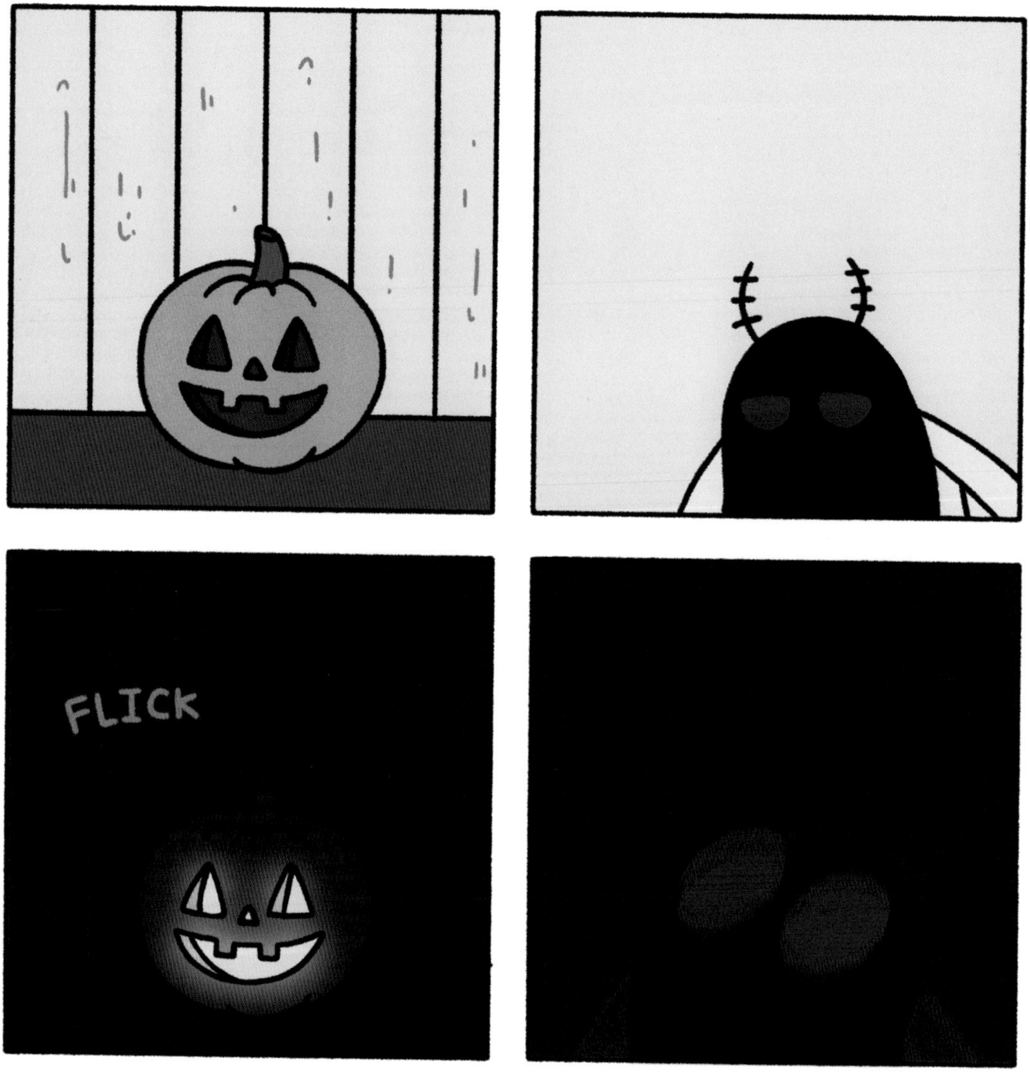
FLICK

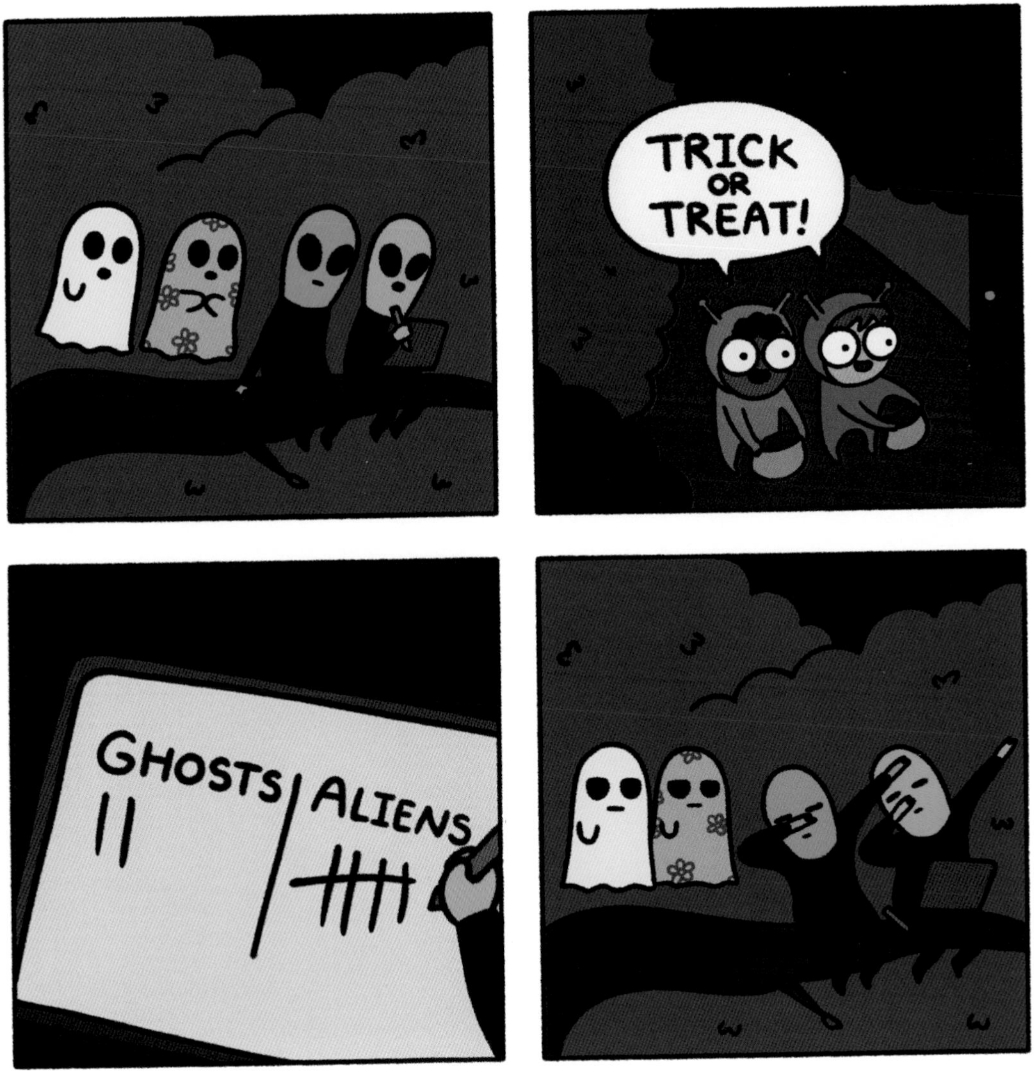
TRICK OR TREAT!
GHOSTS
ALIENS

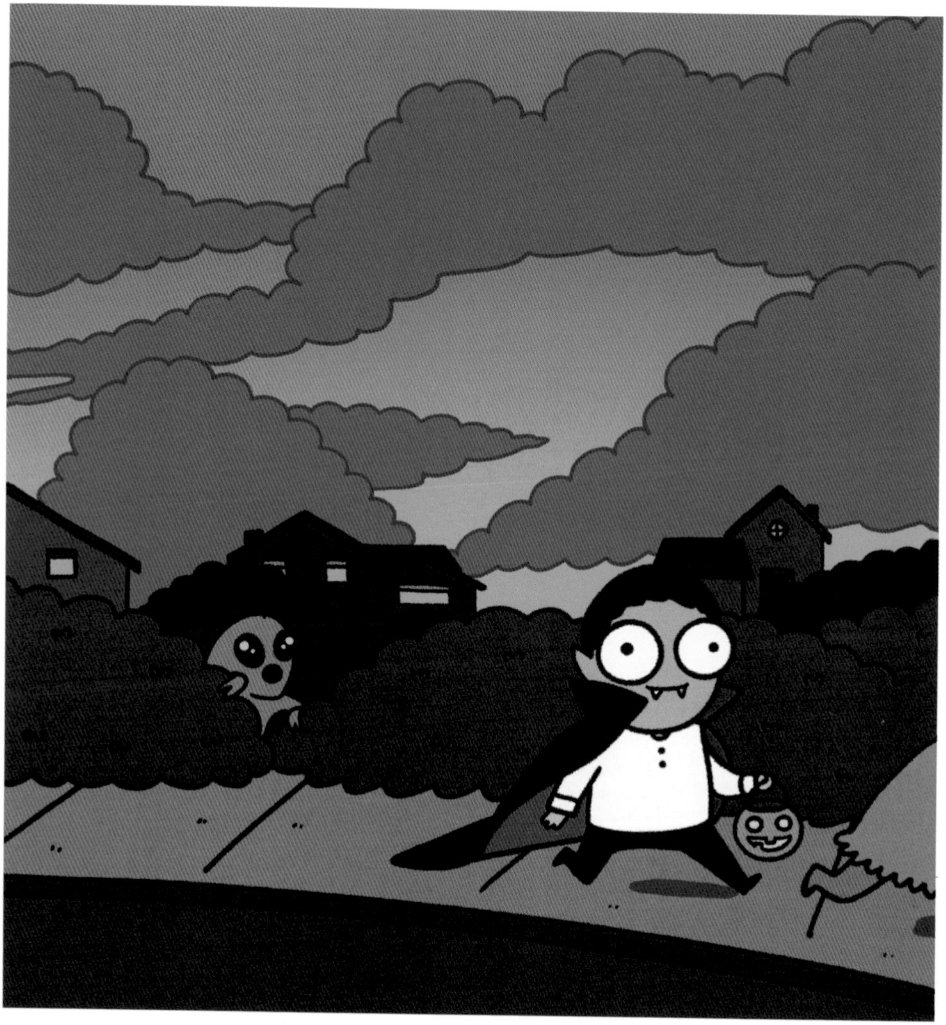

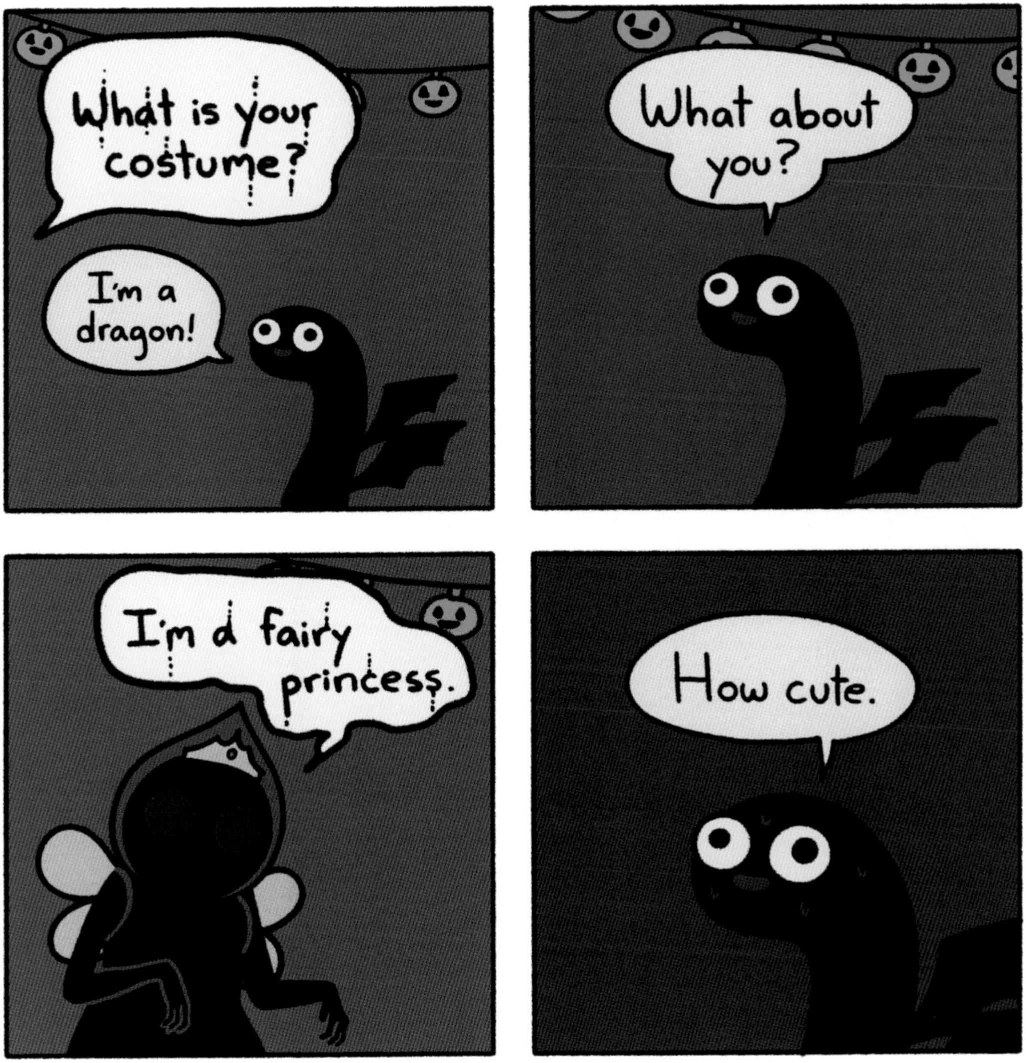
What is your costume?
I'm a dragon!
What about you?
I'm a fairy princess.
How cute.

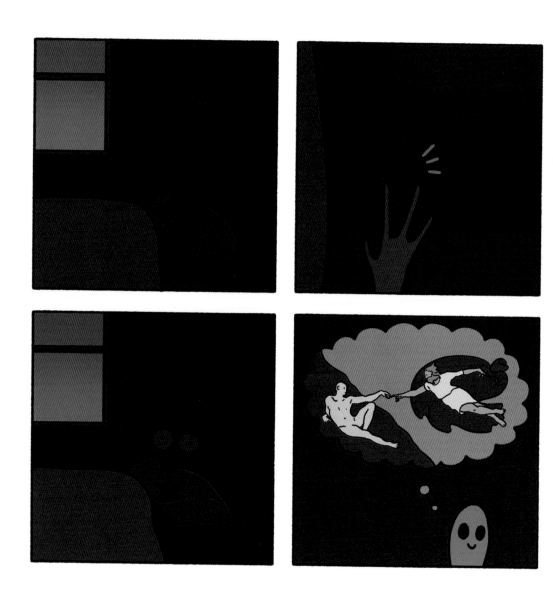

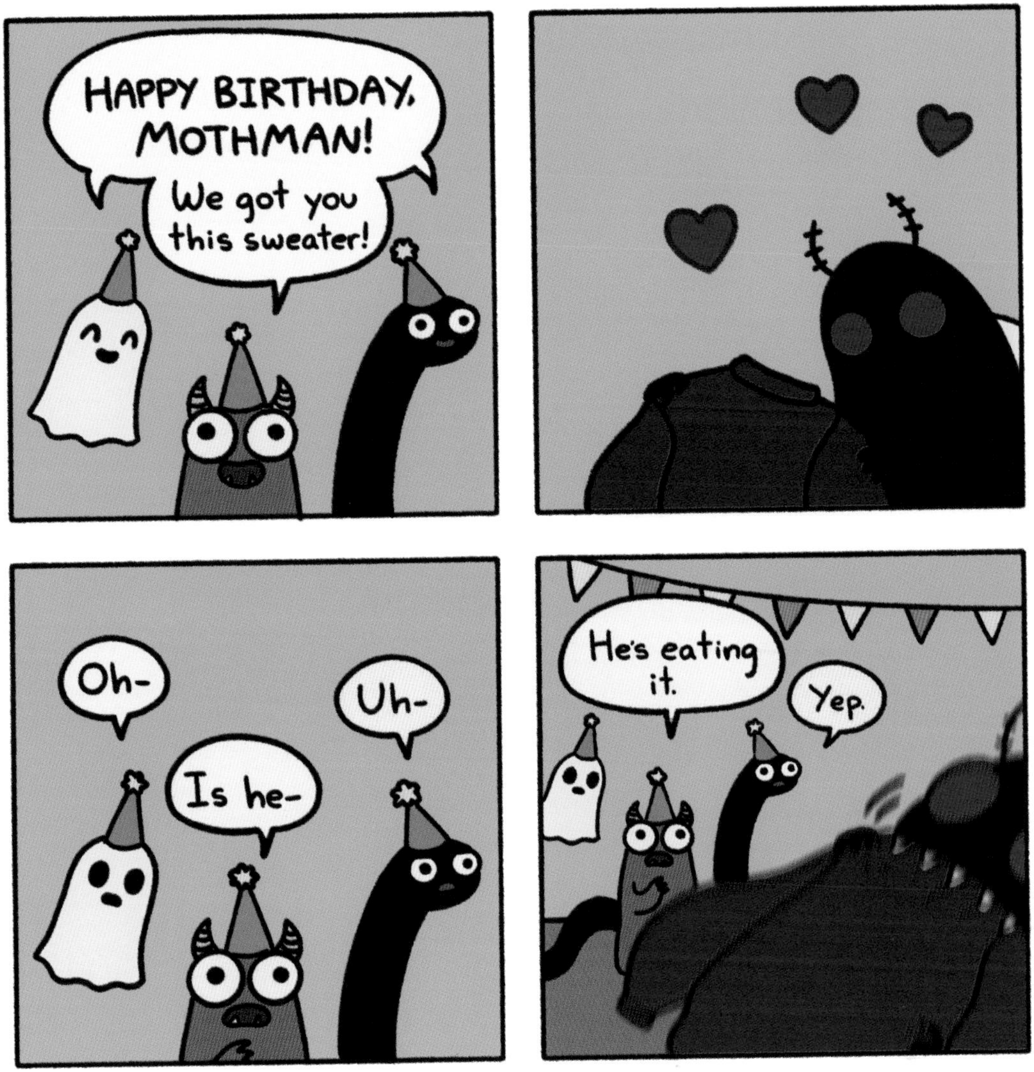
HAPPY BIRTHDAY, MOTHMAN!
We got you this sweater!
Oh-
Is he-
Uh-
He's eating it.
Yep.

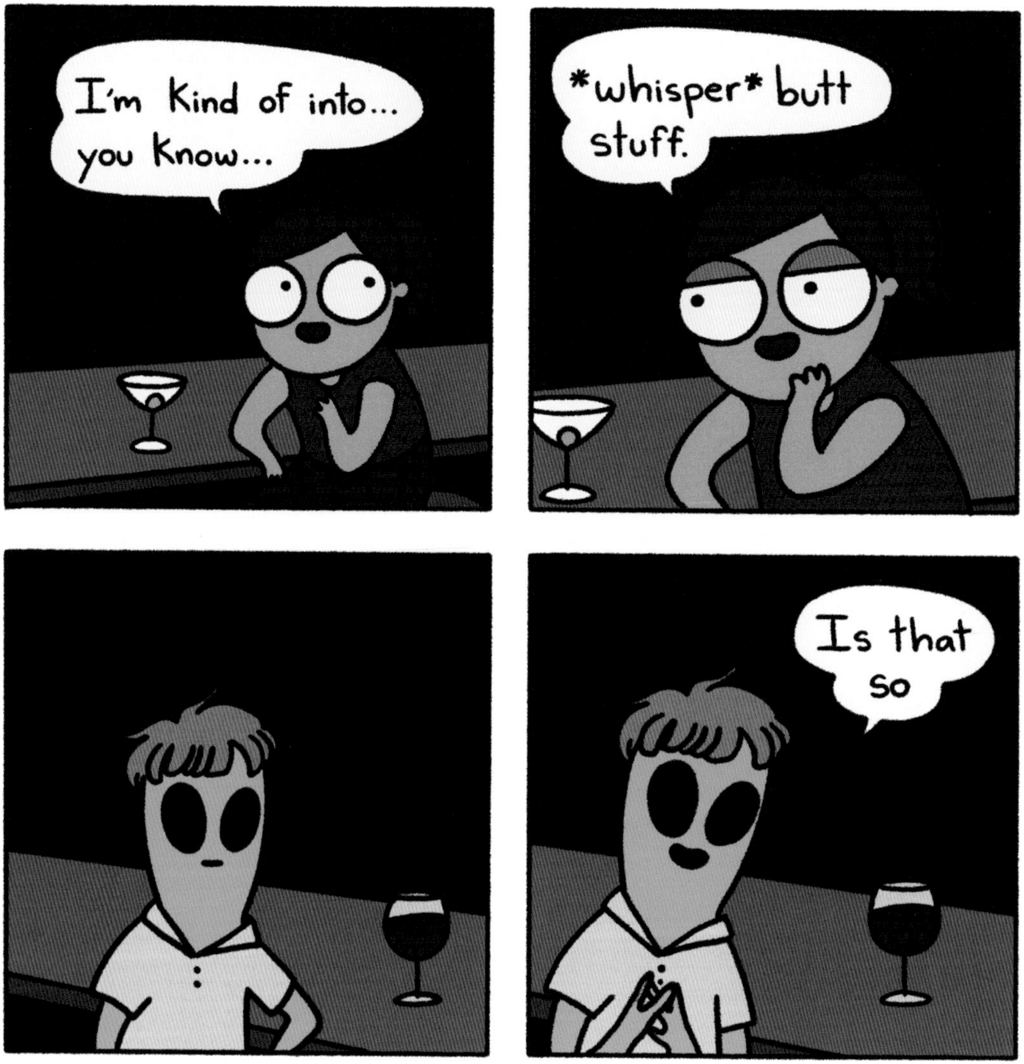
I'm Kind of into... you Know...
whisper butt stuff.
Is that so

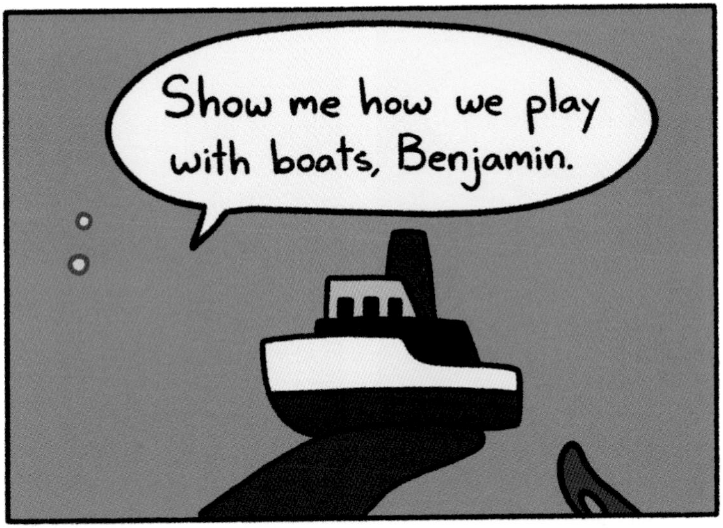
Show me how we play with boats, Benjamin.

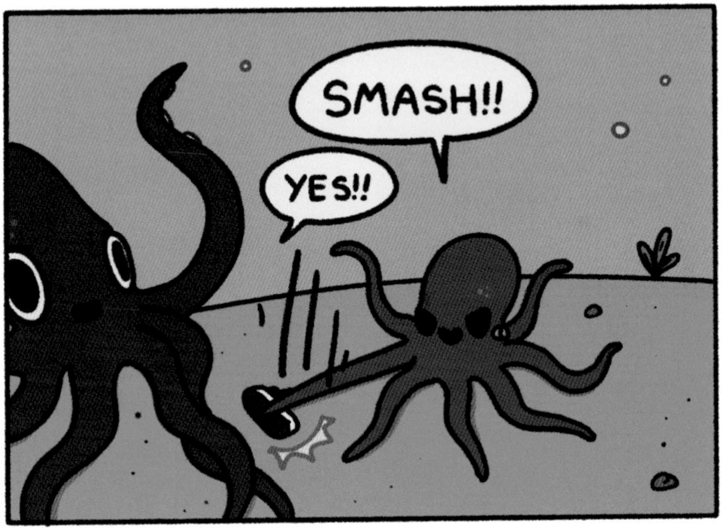
SMASH!!
YES!!

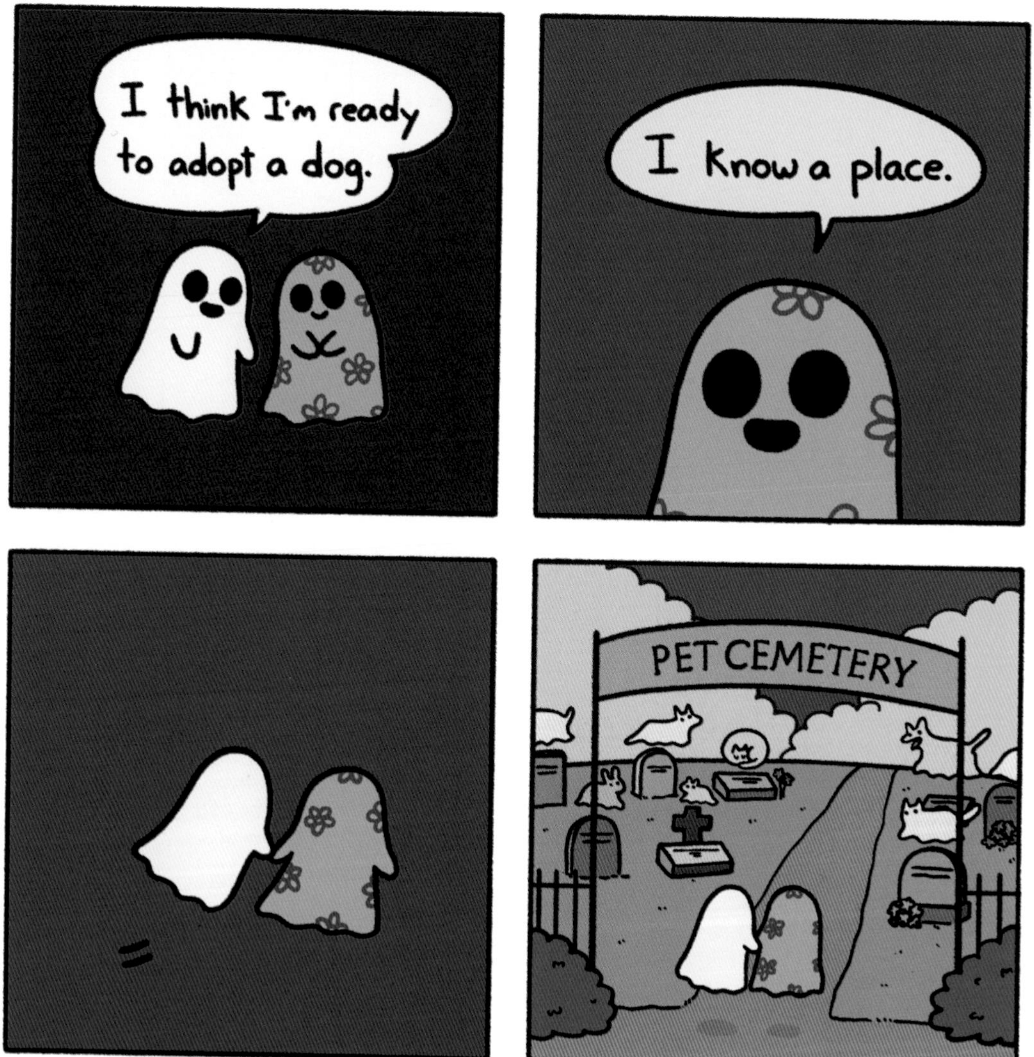
I think I'm ready to adopt a dog.
I know a place.
PET CEMETERY

GIRLS' NIGHT

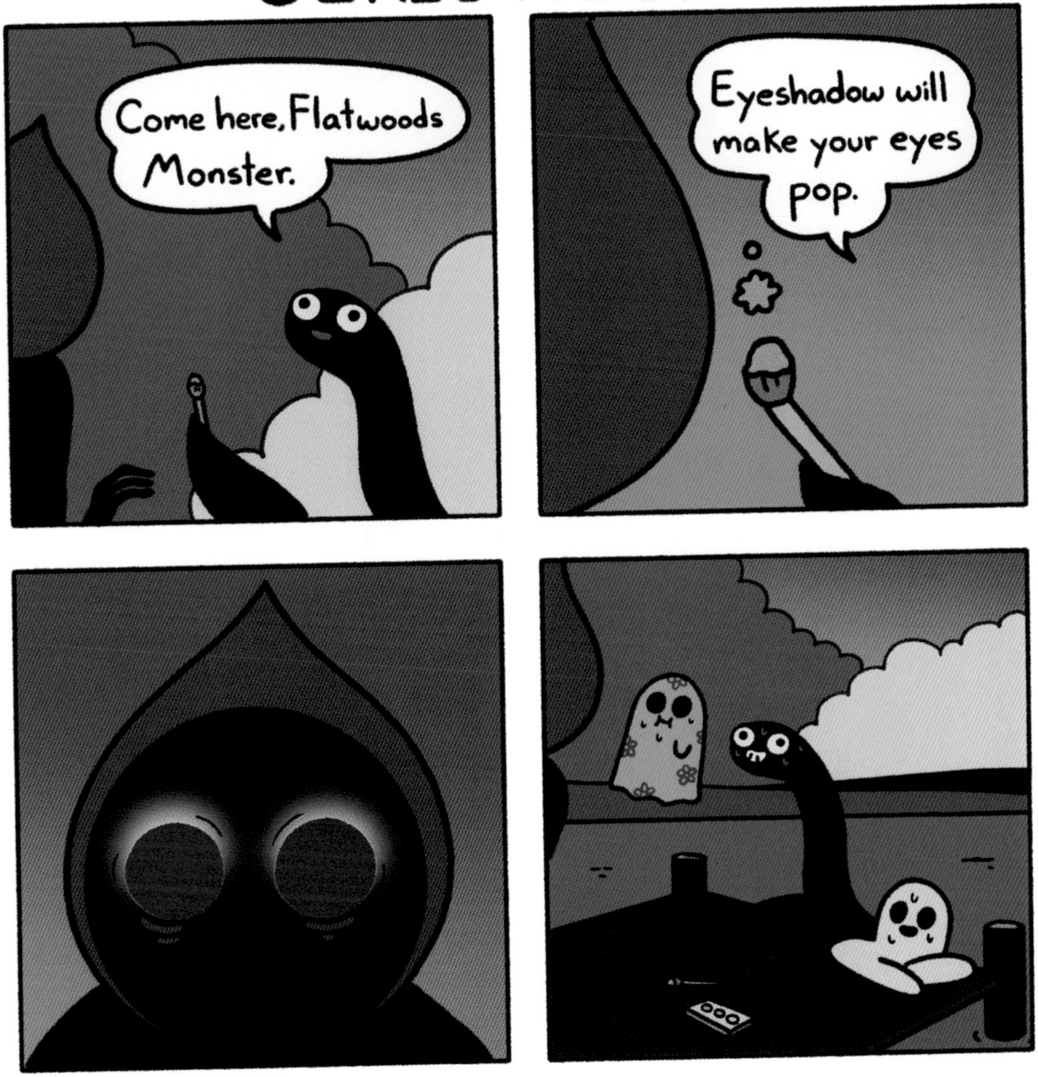
Come here, Flatwoods Monster.
Eyeshadow will make your eyes pop.

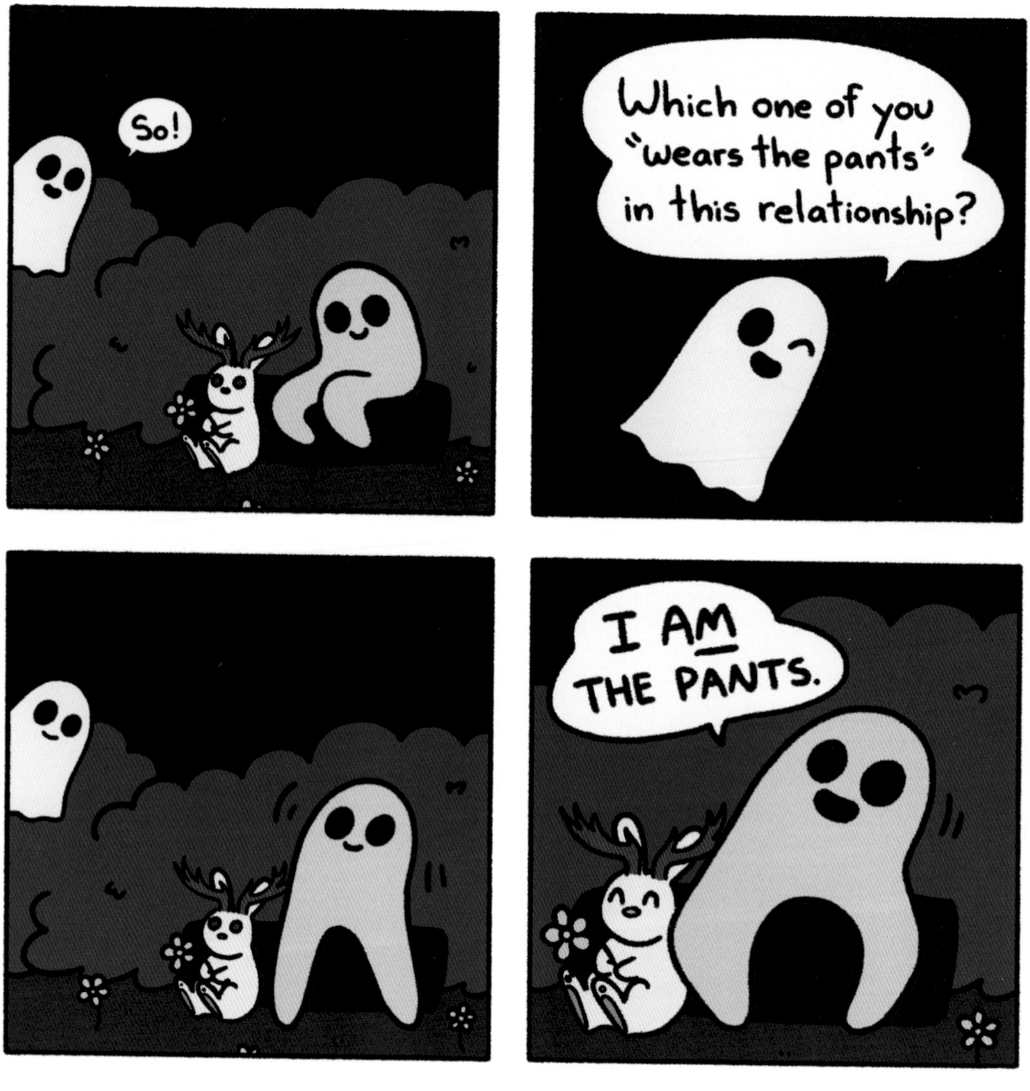
So!
Which one of you "wears the pants" in this relationship?
I AM THE PANTS.

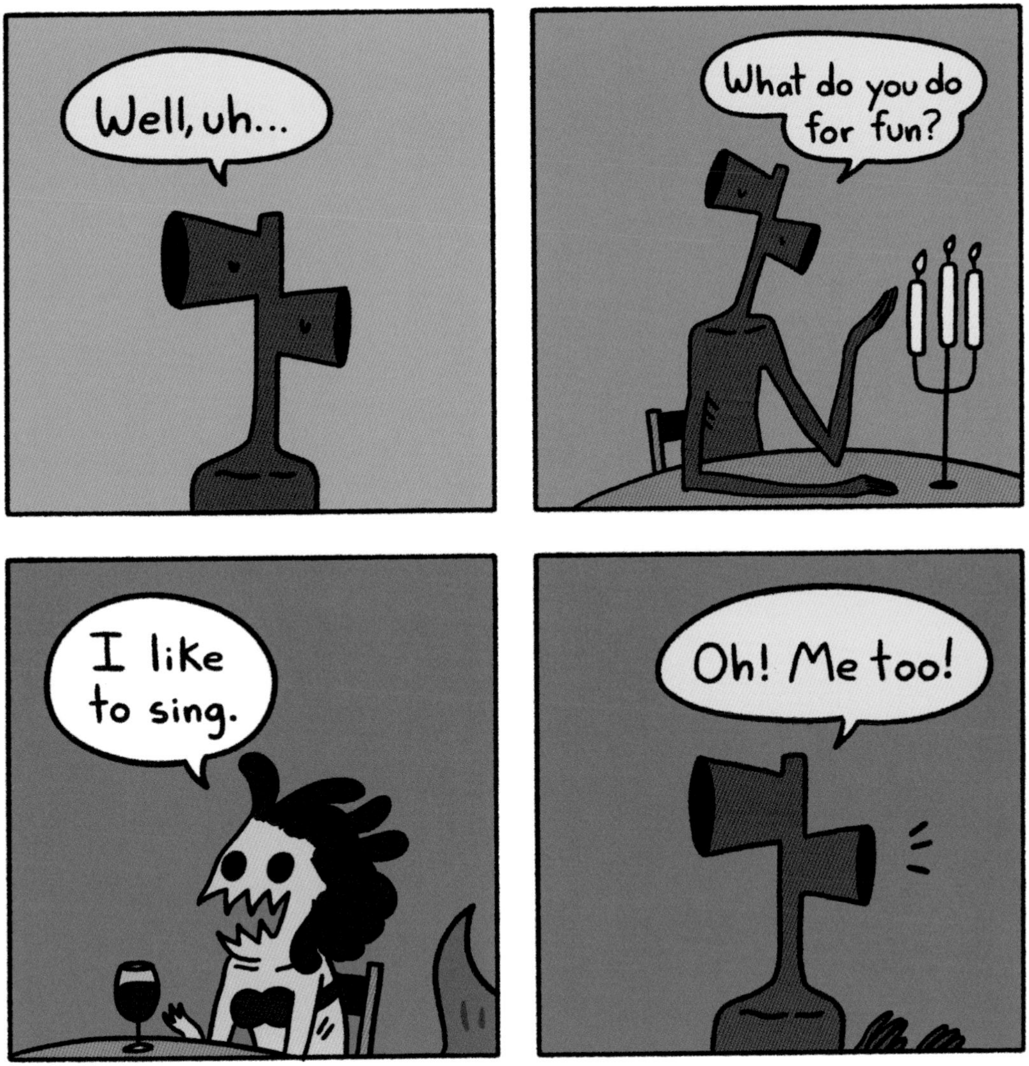
Well, uh...
What do you do for fun?
I like to sing.
Oh! Me too!

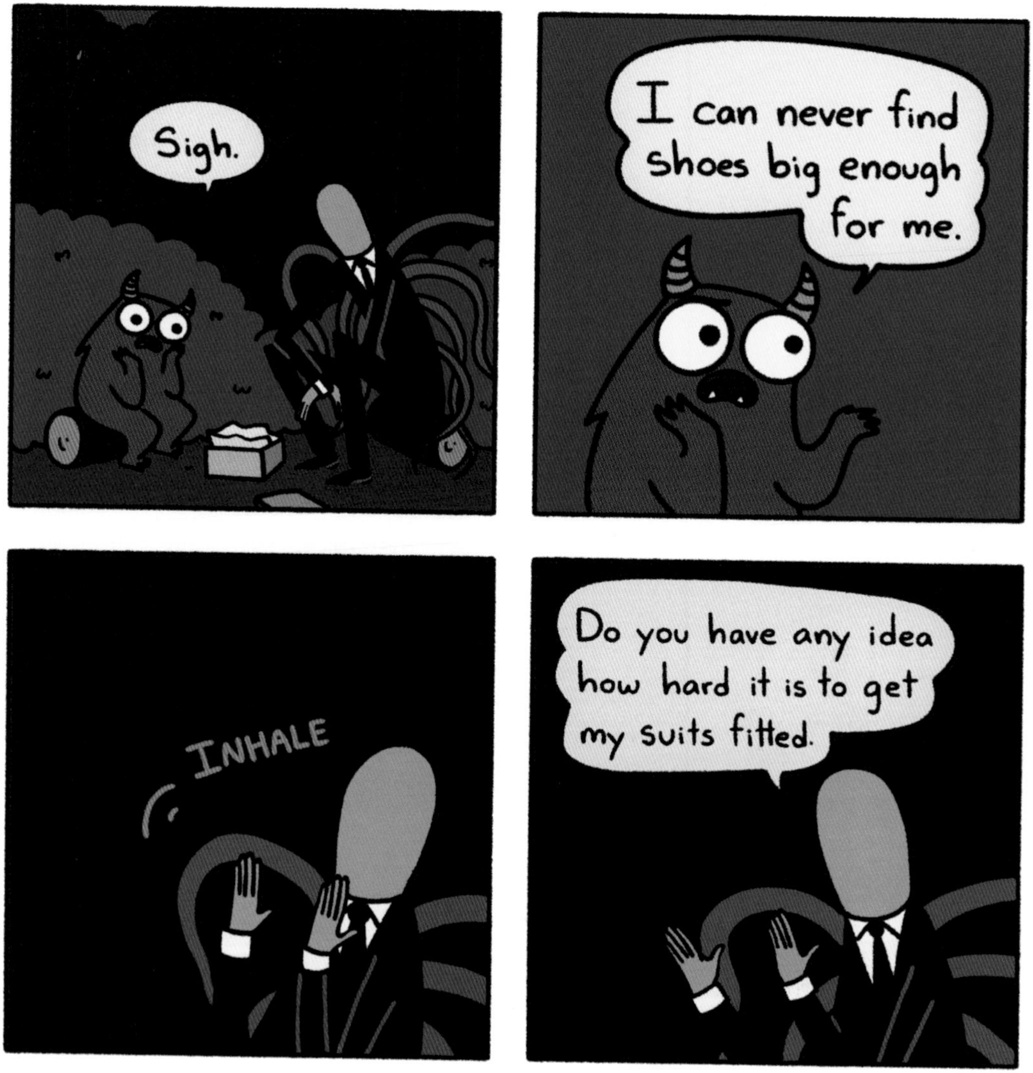
Sigh.
I can never find shoes big enough for me.
INHALE
Do you have any idea how hard it is to get my suits fitted.

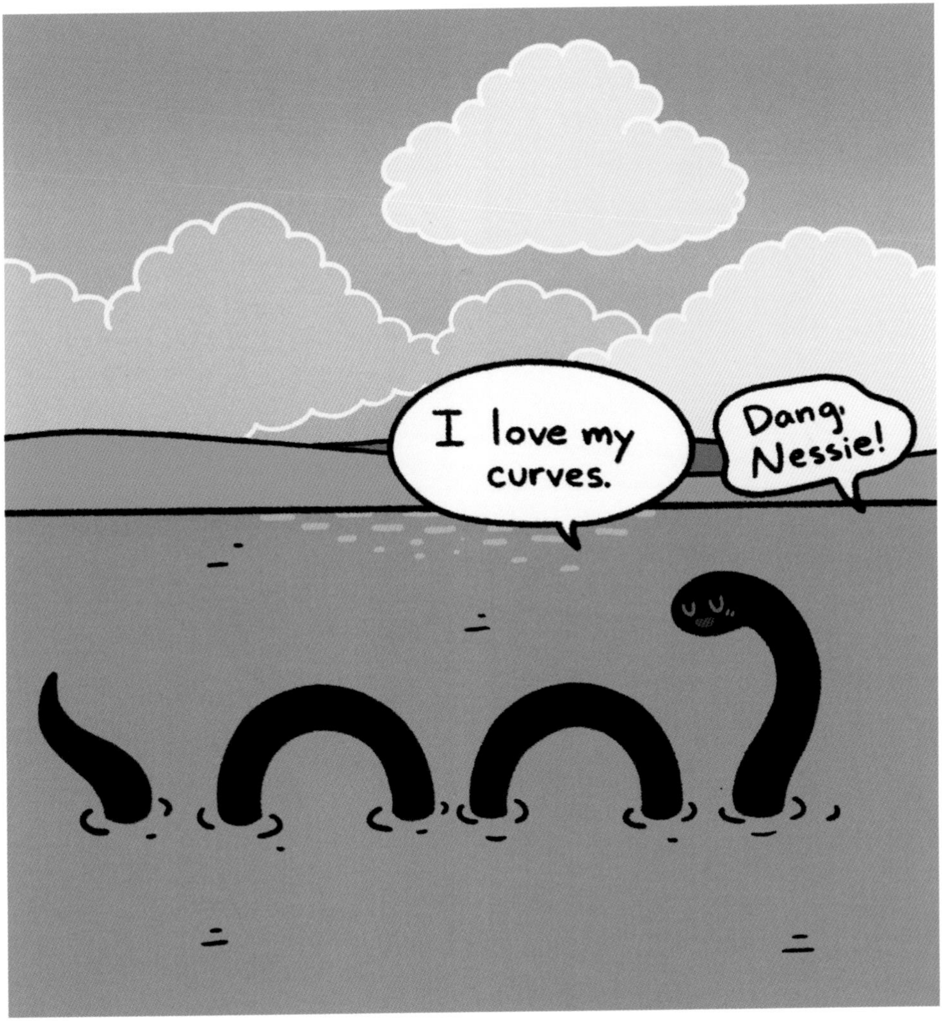
I love my curves.
Dang, Nessie!

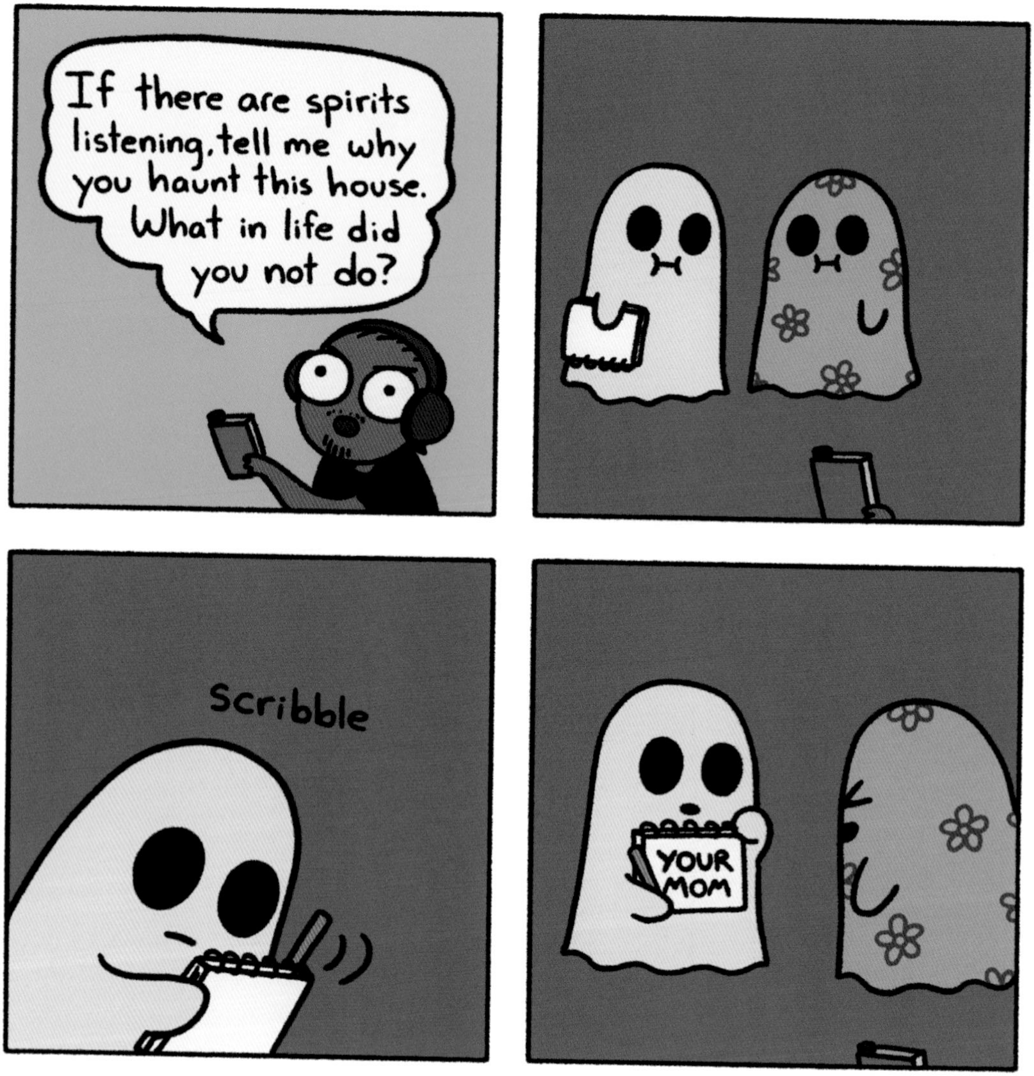
If there are spirits listening, tell me why you haunt this house. What in life did you not do?
scribble
YOUR MOM

PAPARAZZI

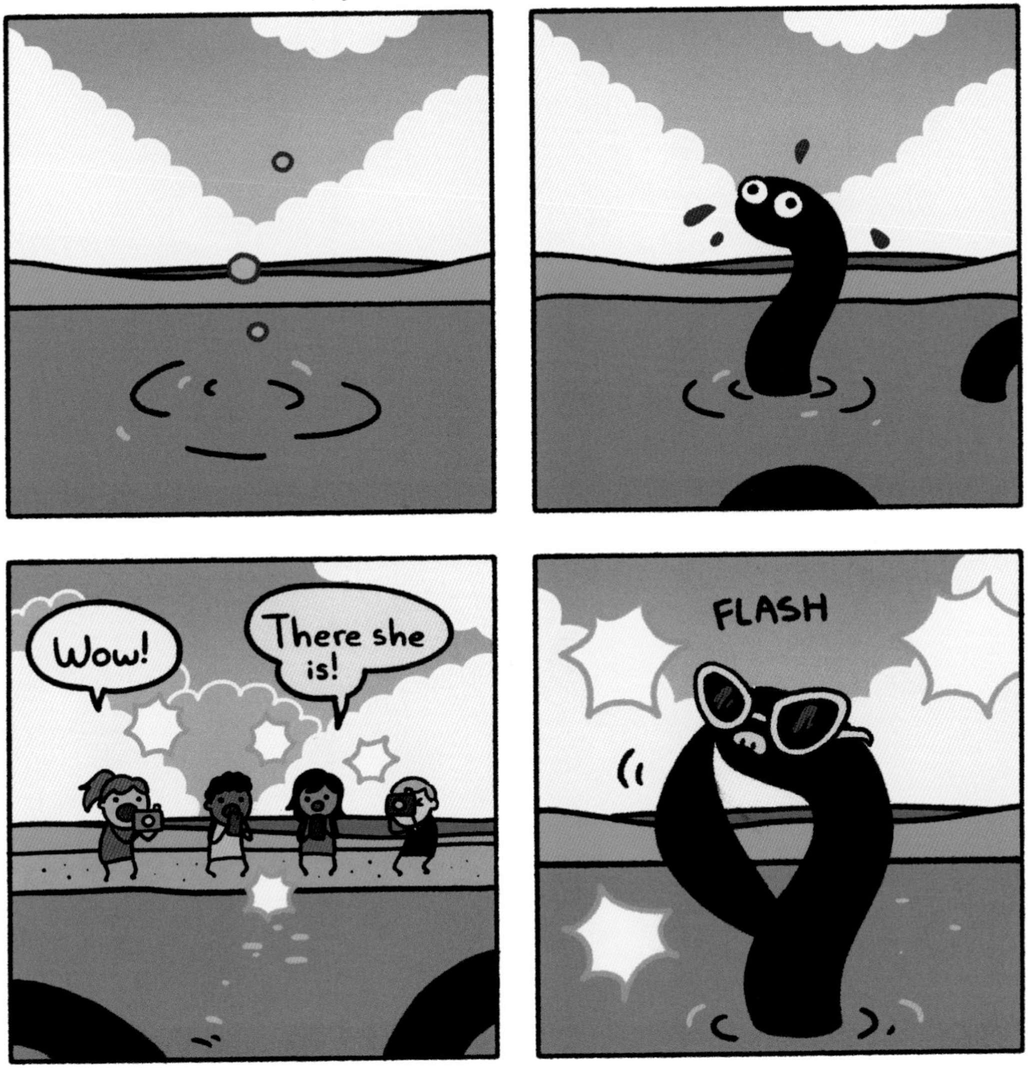

Wow!
There she is!
FLASH

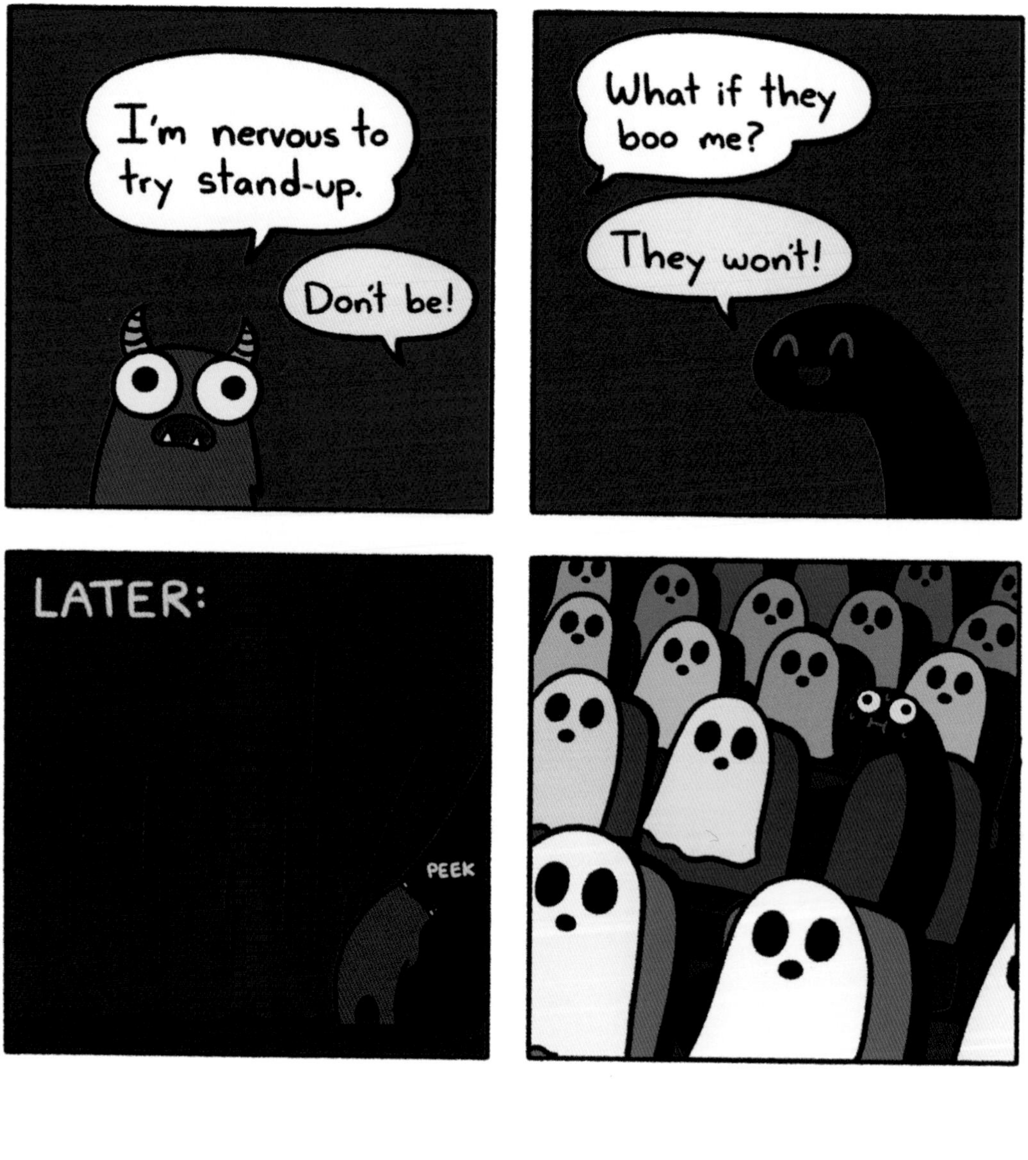
I'm nervous to try stand-up.
Don't be!
What if they boo me?
They won't!
LATER:
PEEK

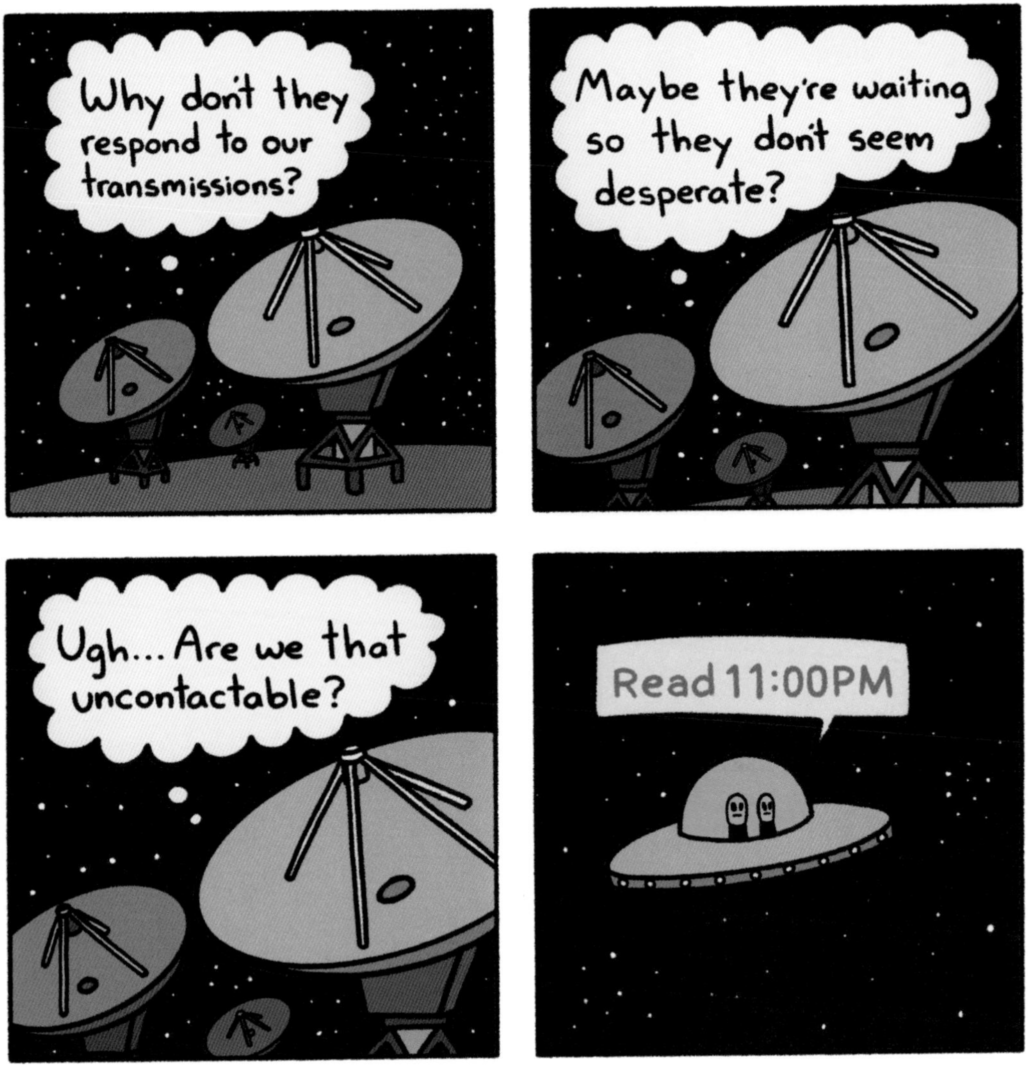
Why don't they respond to our transmissions?
Maybe they're waiting so they don't seem desperate?
Ugh... Are we that uncontactable?
Read 11:00PM

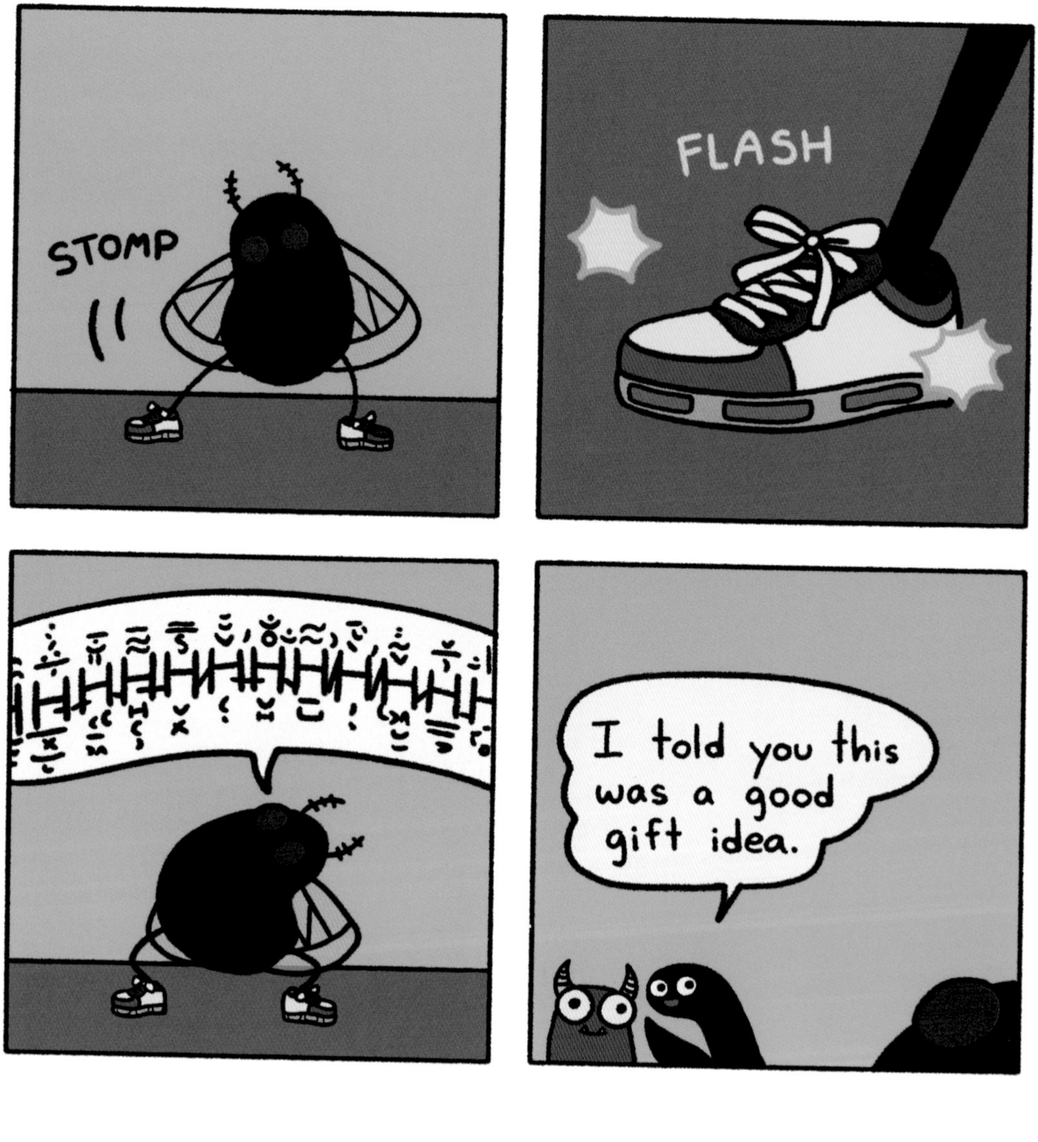
STOMP
FLASH
I told you this was a good gift idea.

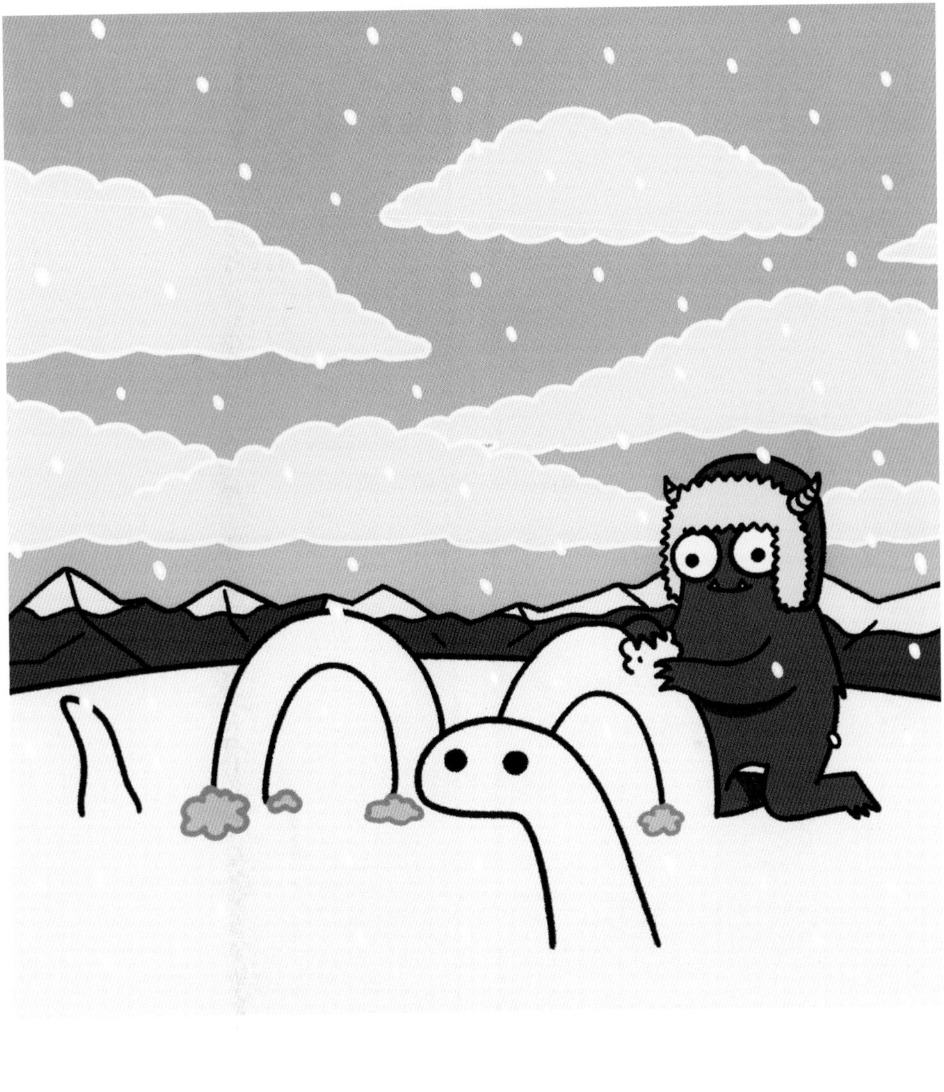

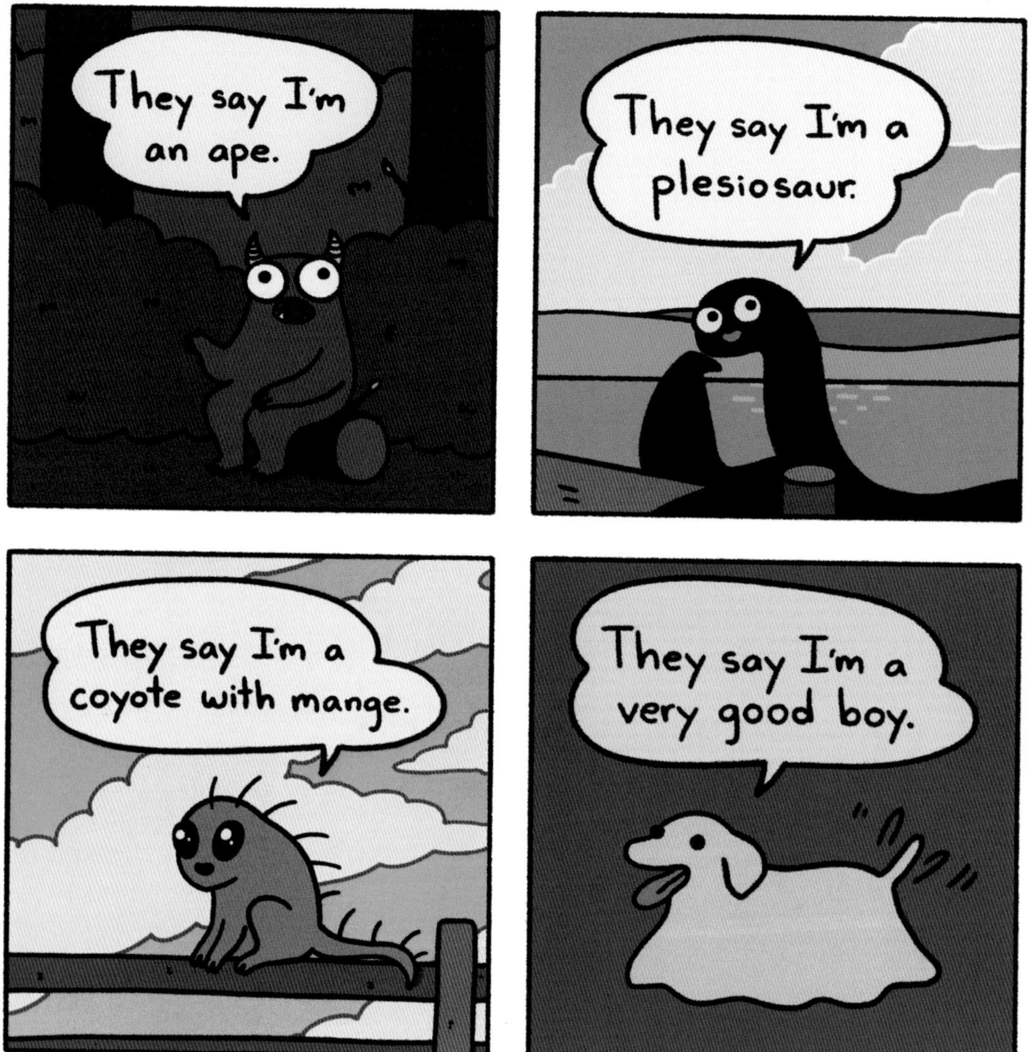
They say I'm an ape.
They say I'm a plesiosaur.
They say I'm a coyote with mange.
They say I'm a very good boy.

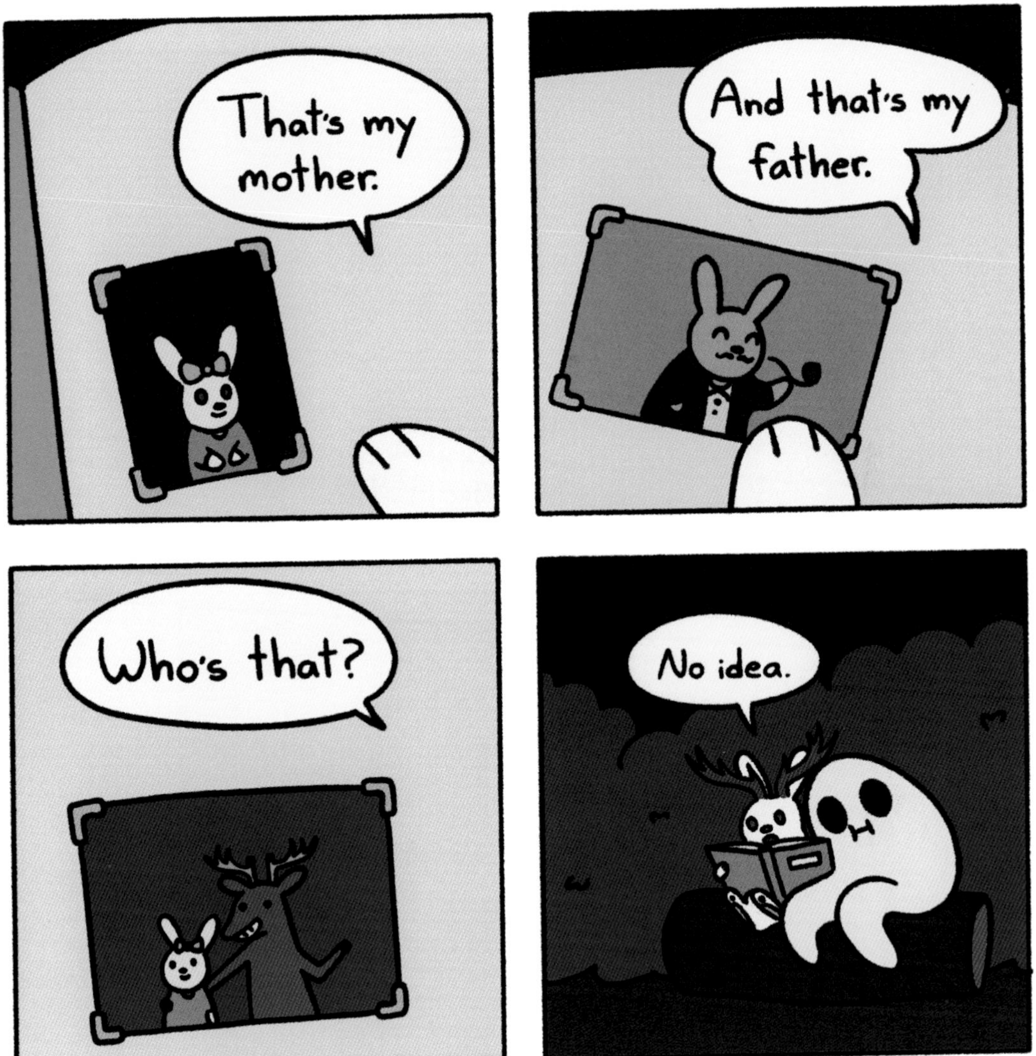
That's my mother.
And that's my father.
Who's that?
No idea.

STARING CONTEST

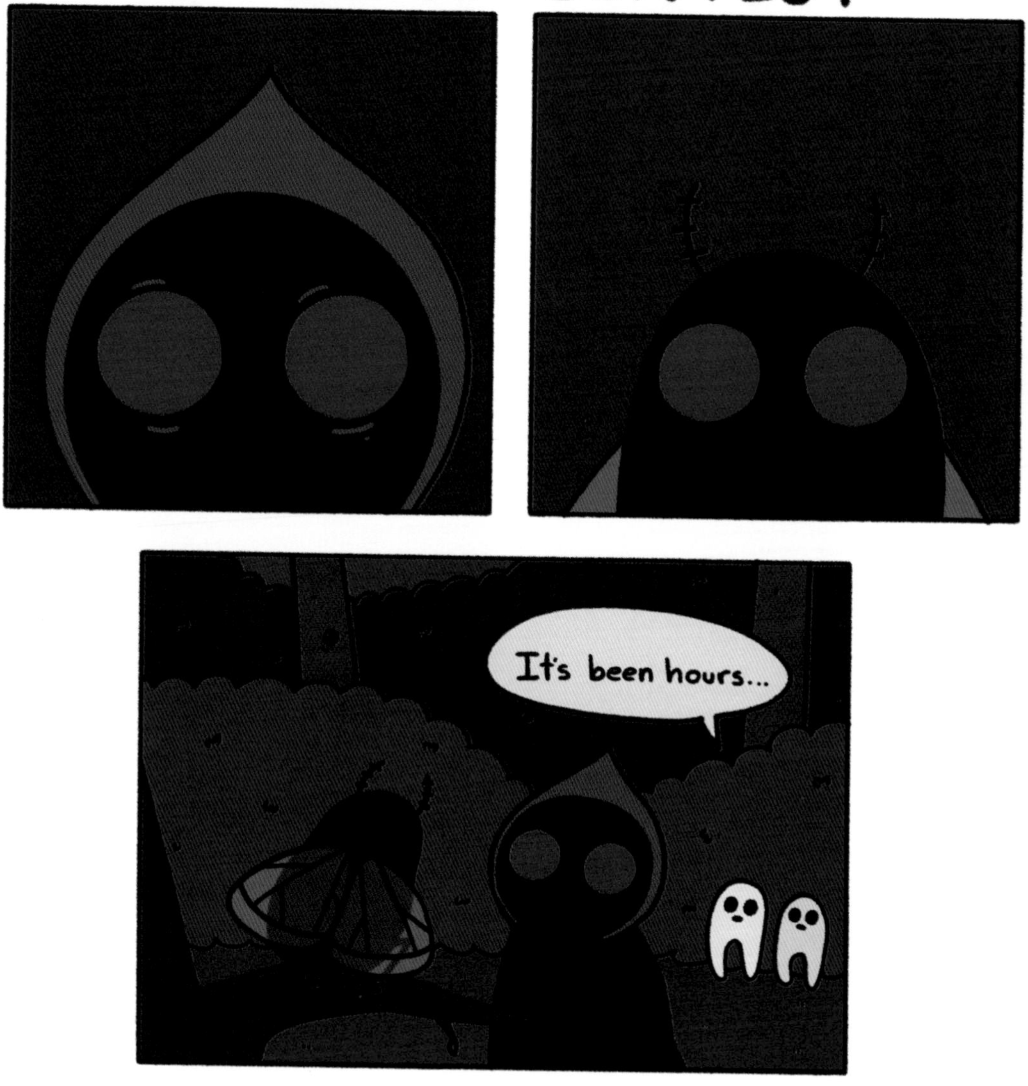
It's been hours...

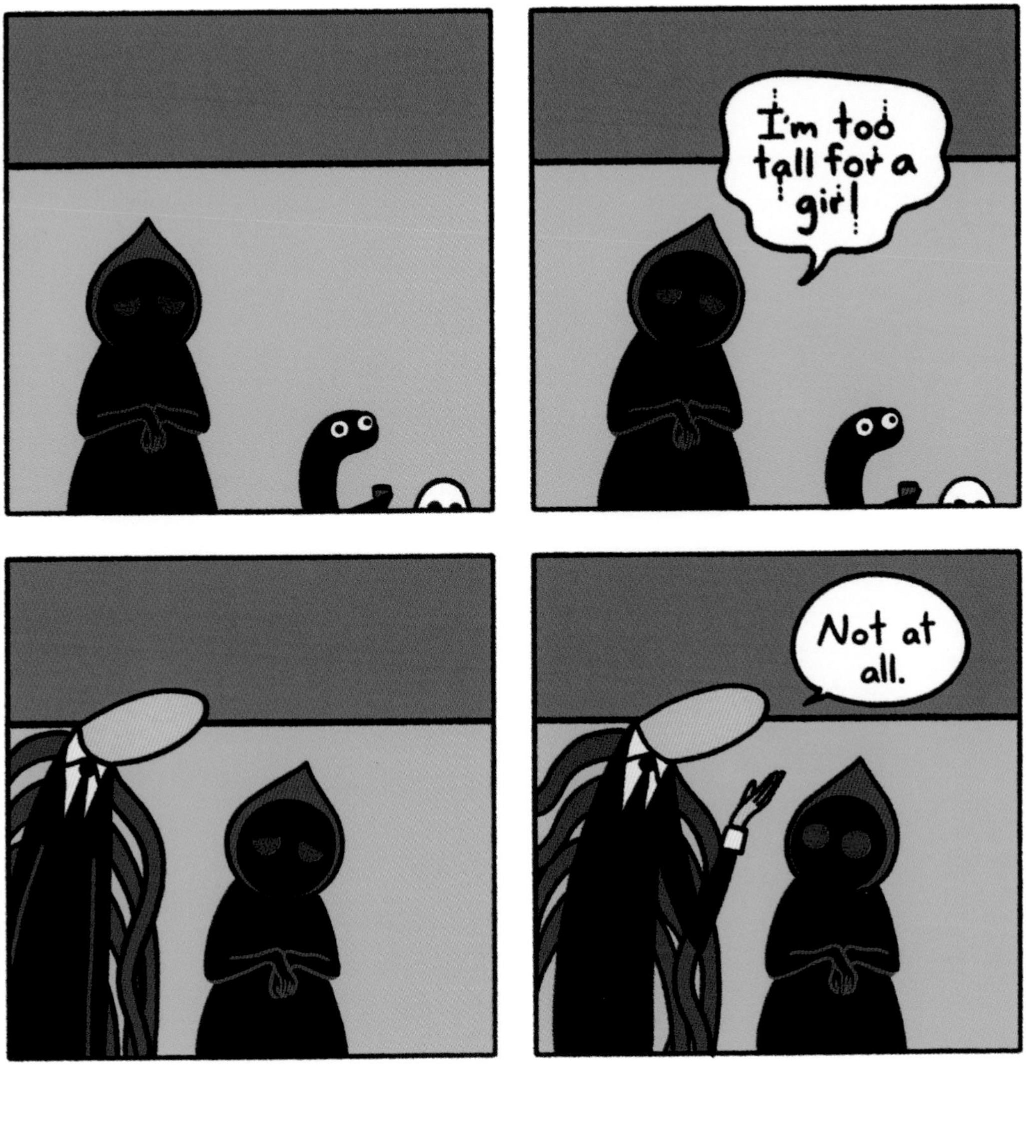
I'm too tall for a girl!
Not at all.

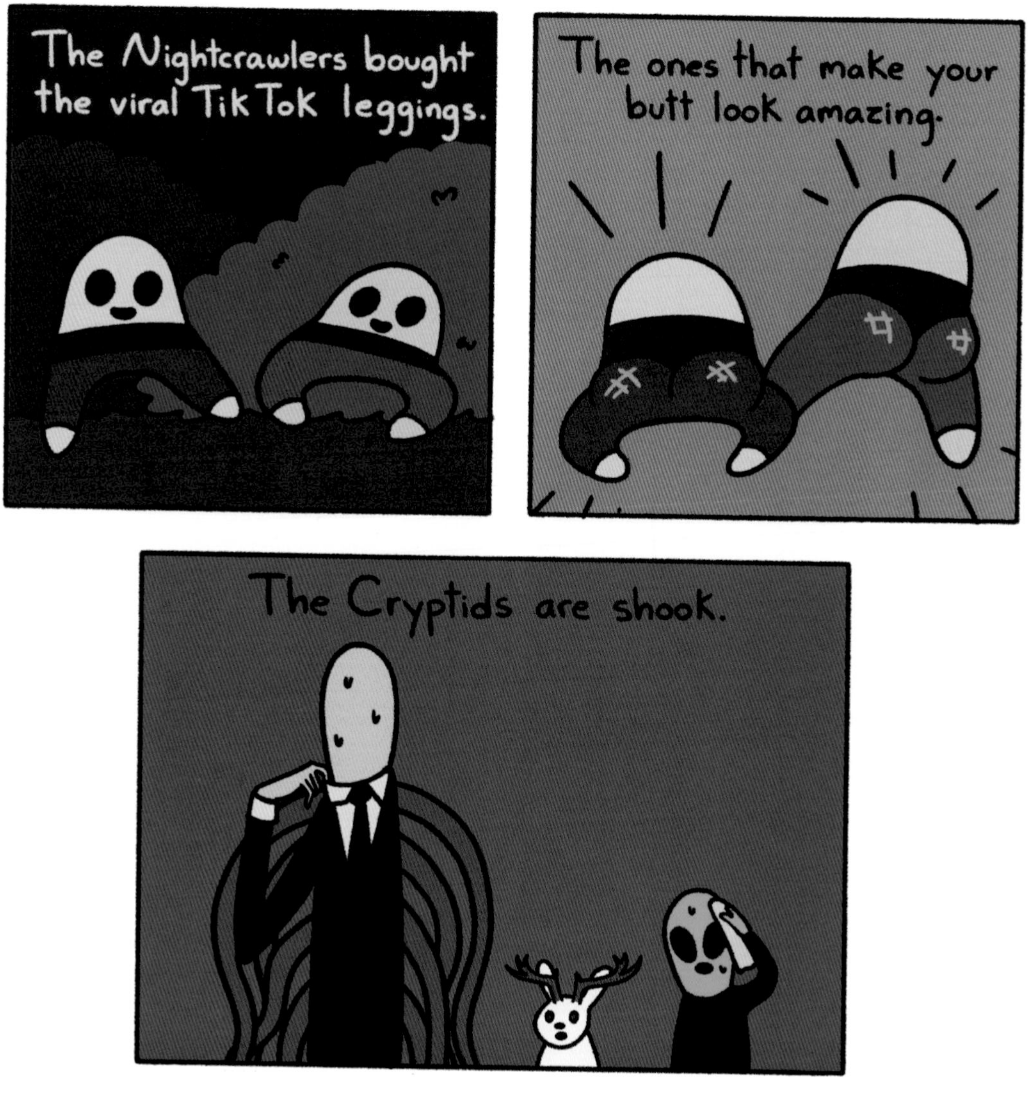
The Nightcrawlers bought the viral TikTok leggings.
The ones that make your butt look amazing.
The Cryptids are shook.

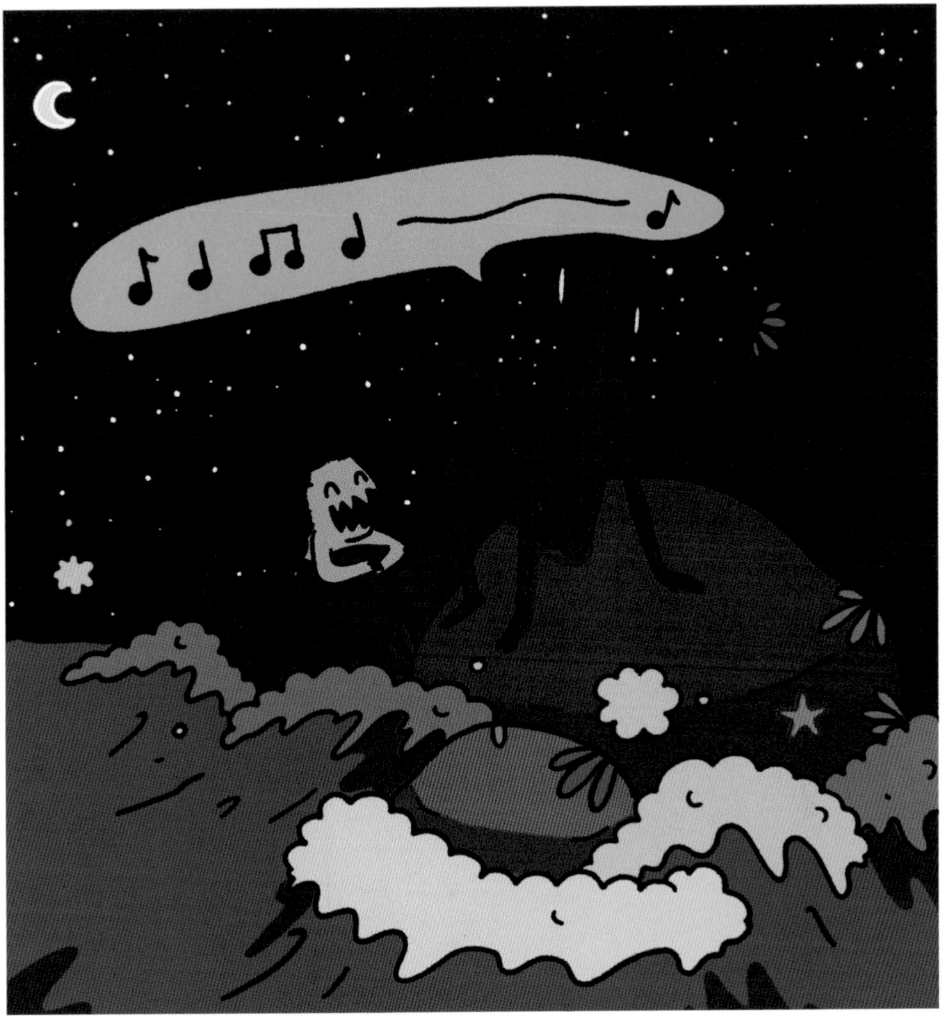

CRYPTID VALENTINES

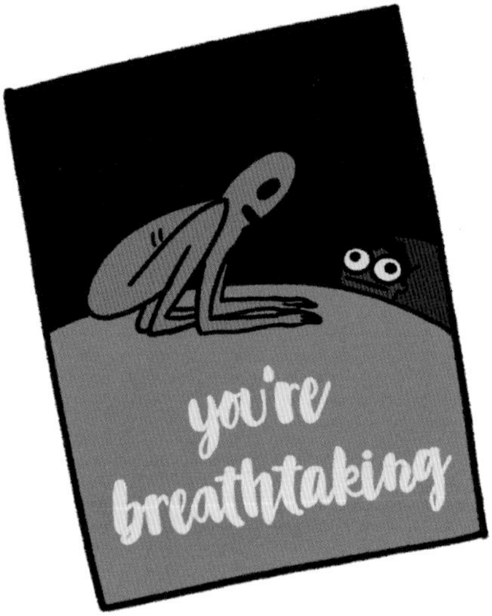
you're breathtaking

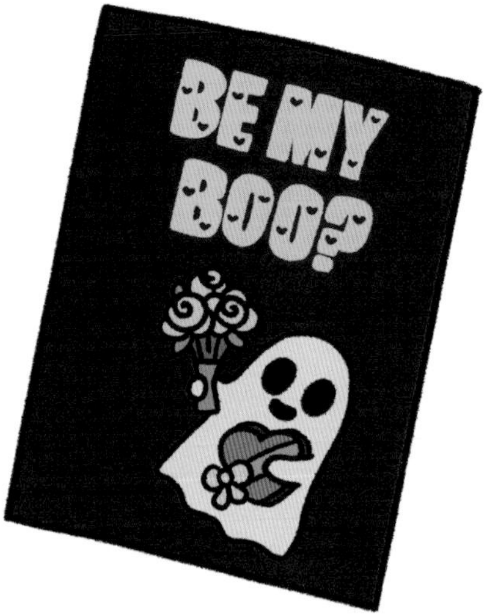
BE MY BOO?

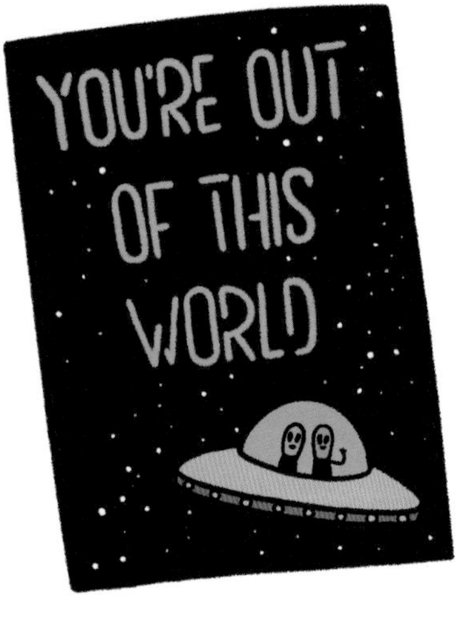
YOU'RE OUT OF THIS WORLD

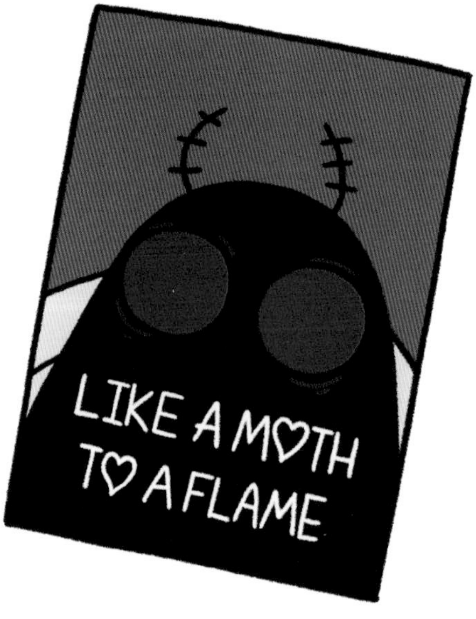
LIKE A MOTH TO A FLAME

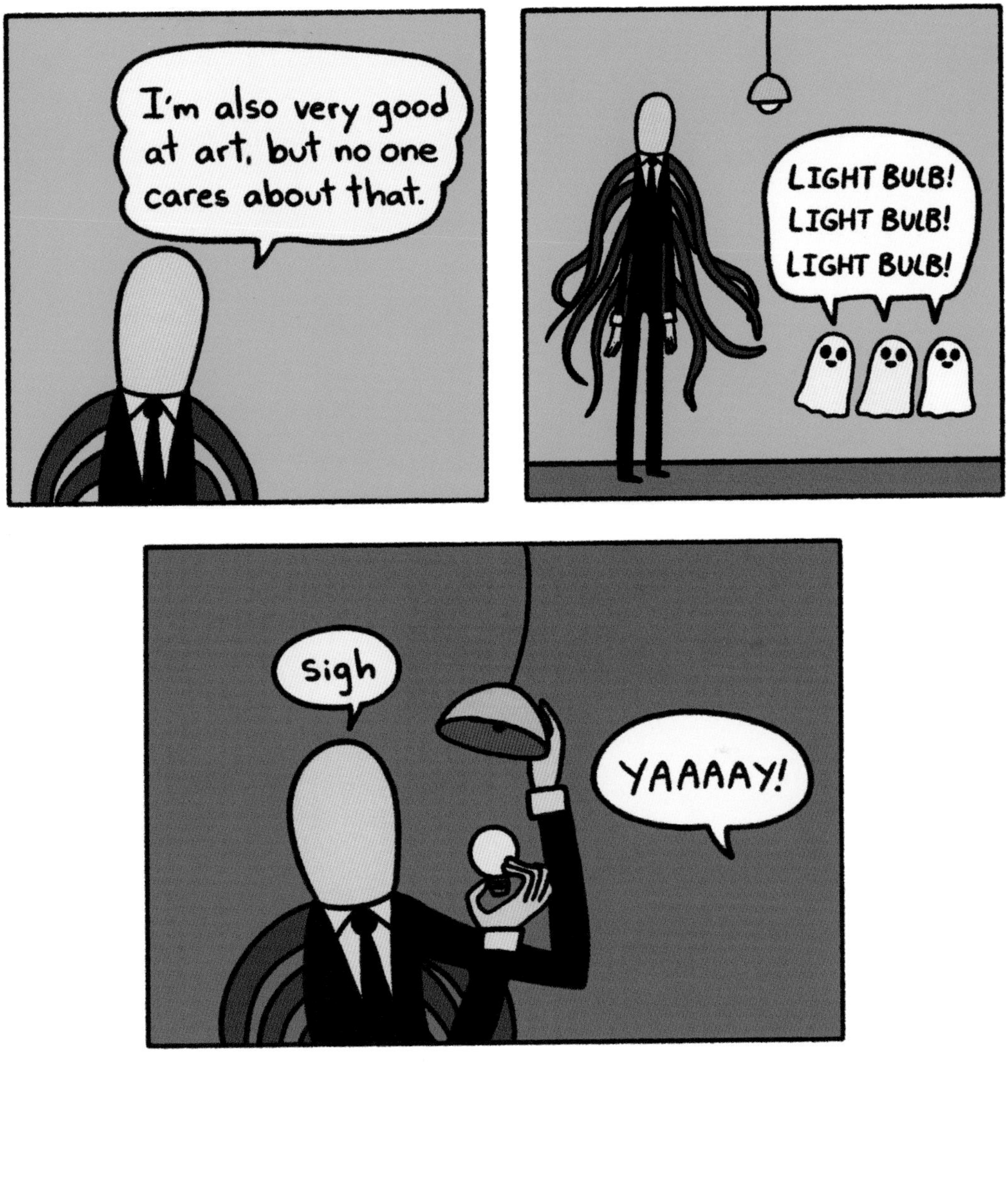
I'm also very good at art, but no one cares about that.
LIGHT BULB! LIGHT BULB! LIGHT BULB!
sigh
YAAAAY!

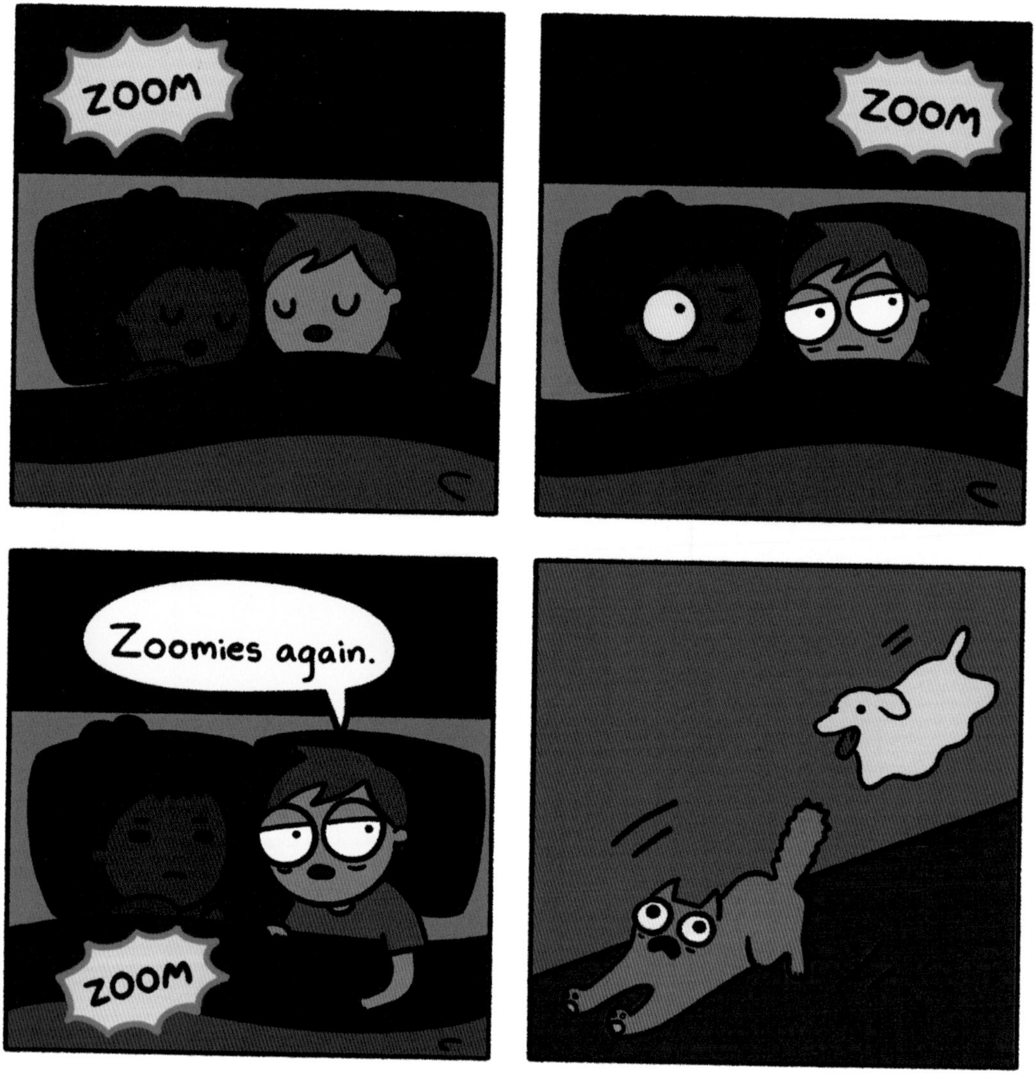
ZOOM
ZOOM
Zoomies again.
ZOOM

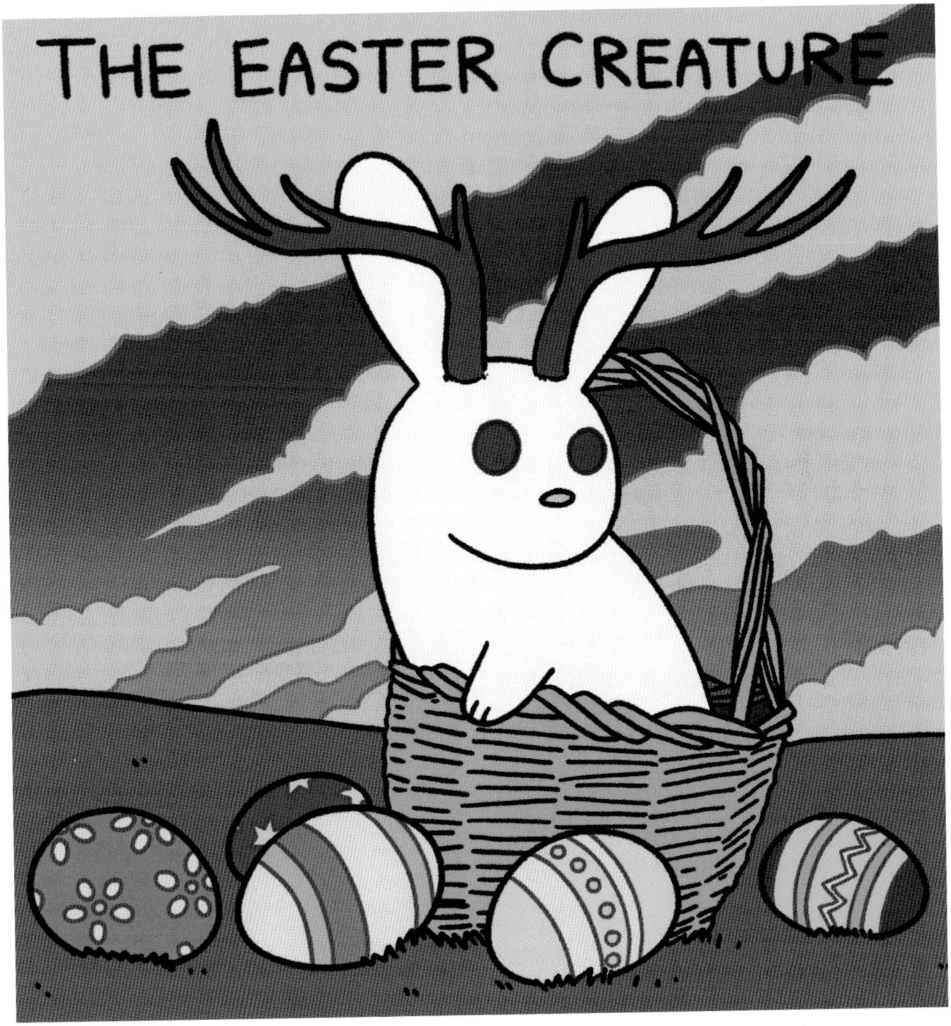
THE EASTER CREATURE

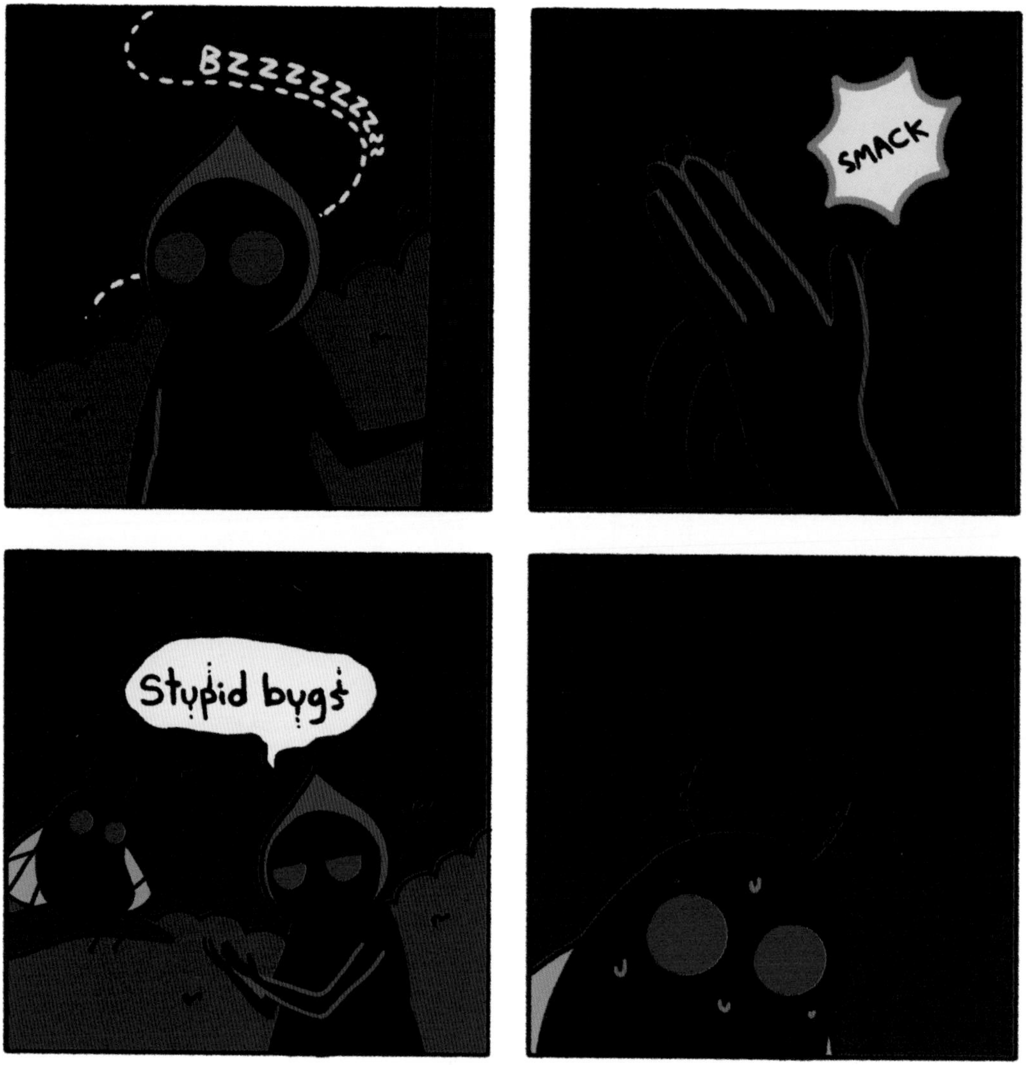
BZZZZZZZZZZ
SMACK
Stupid bugs

POLTERGEIST

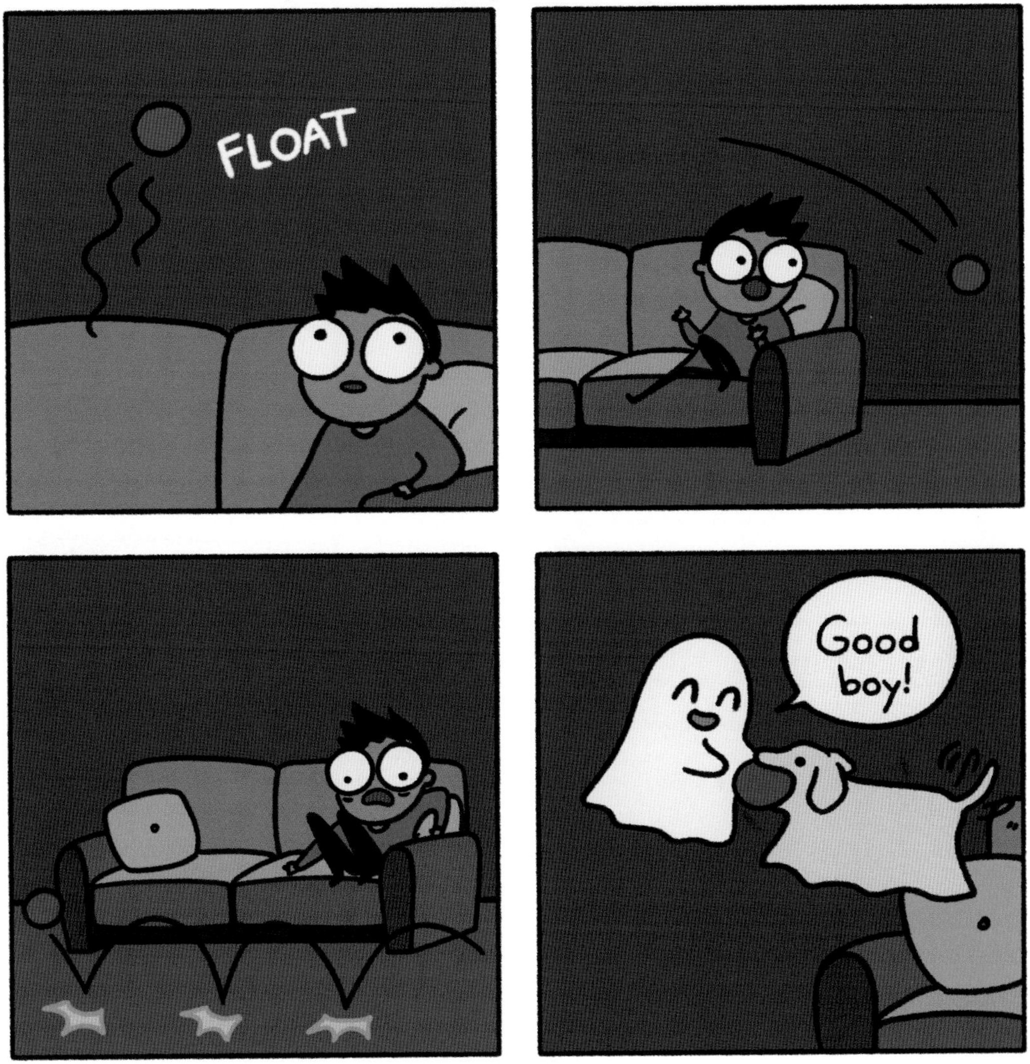
FLOAT
Good boy!

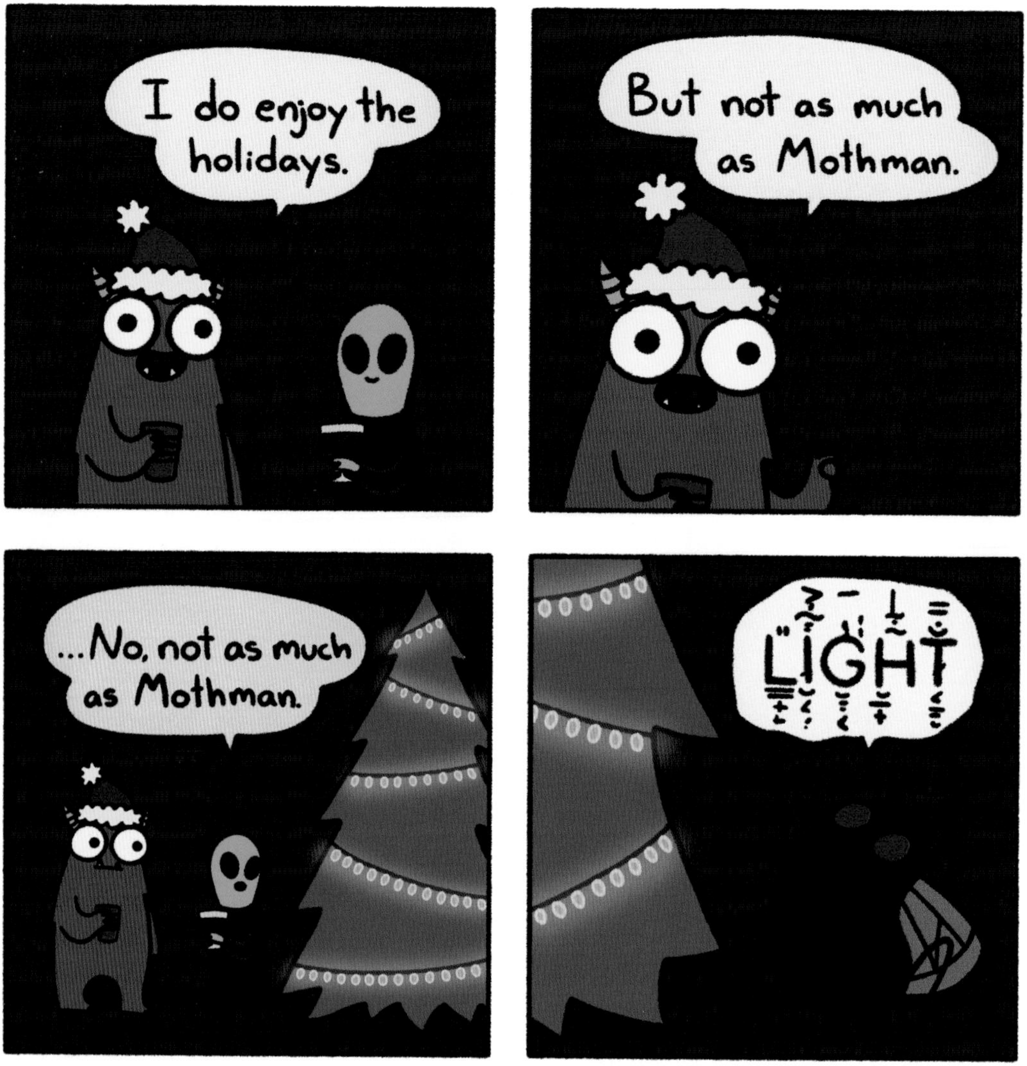
I do enjoy the holidays.
But not as much as Mothman.
...No, not as much as Mothman.
LIGHT

Till death do us part.
Wait–

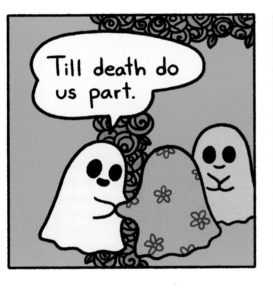

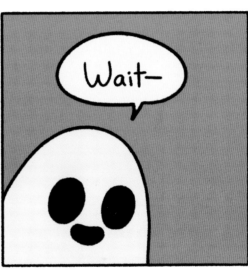

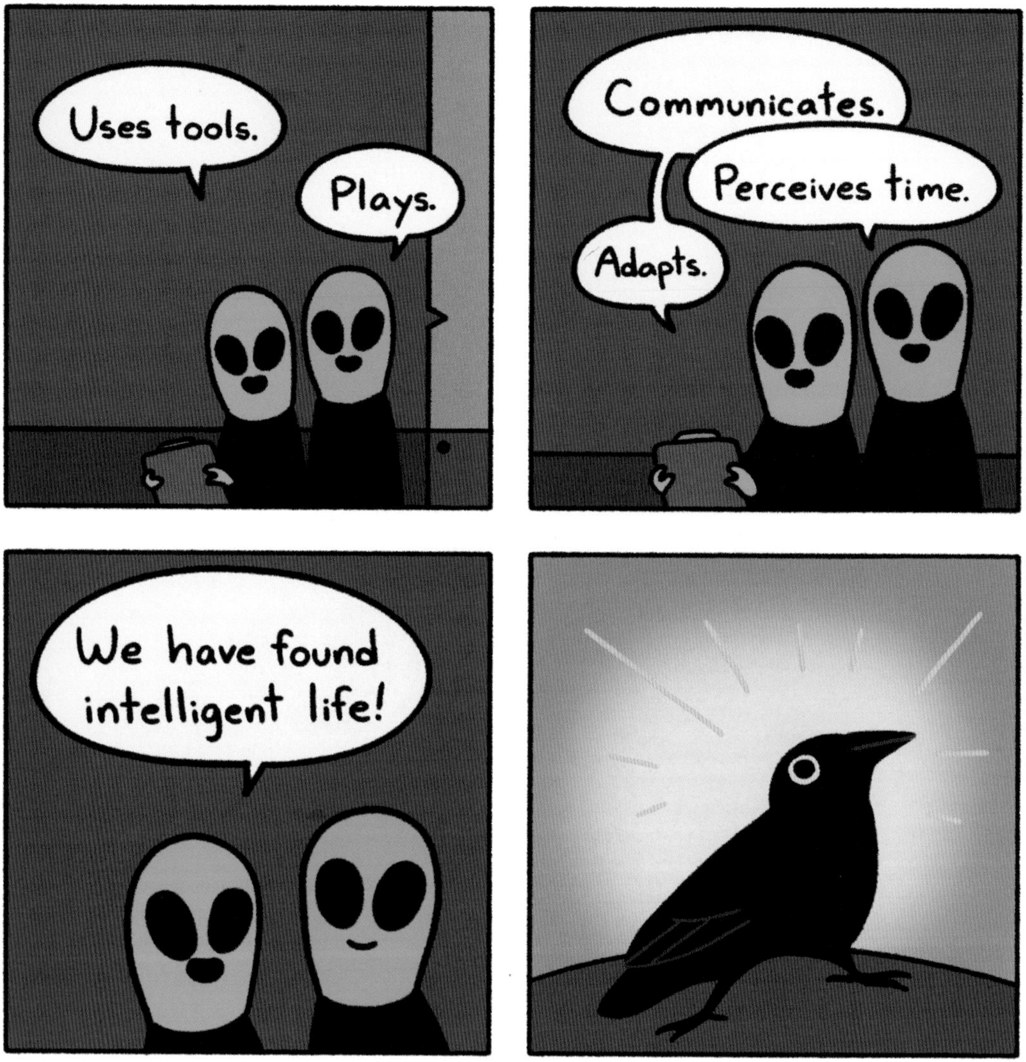
Uses tools.
Plays.
Communicates.
Perceives time.
Adapts.
We have found intelligent life!

NO ARMS? NO PROBLEM

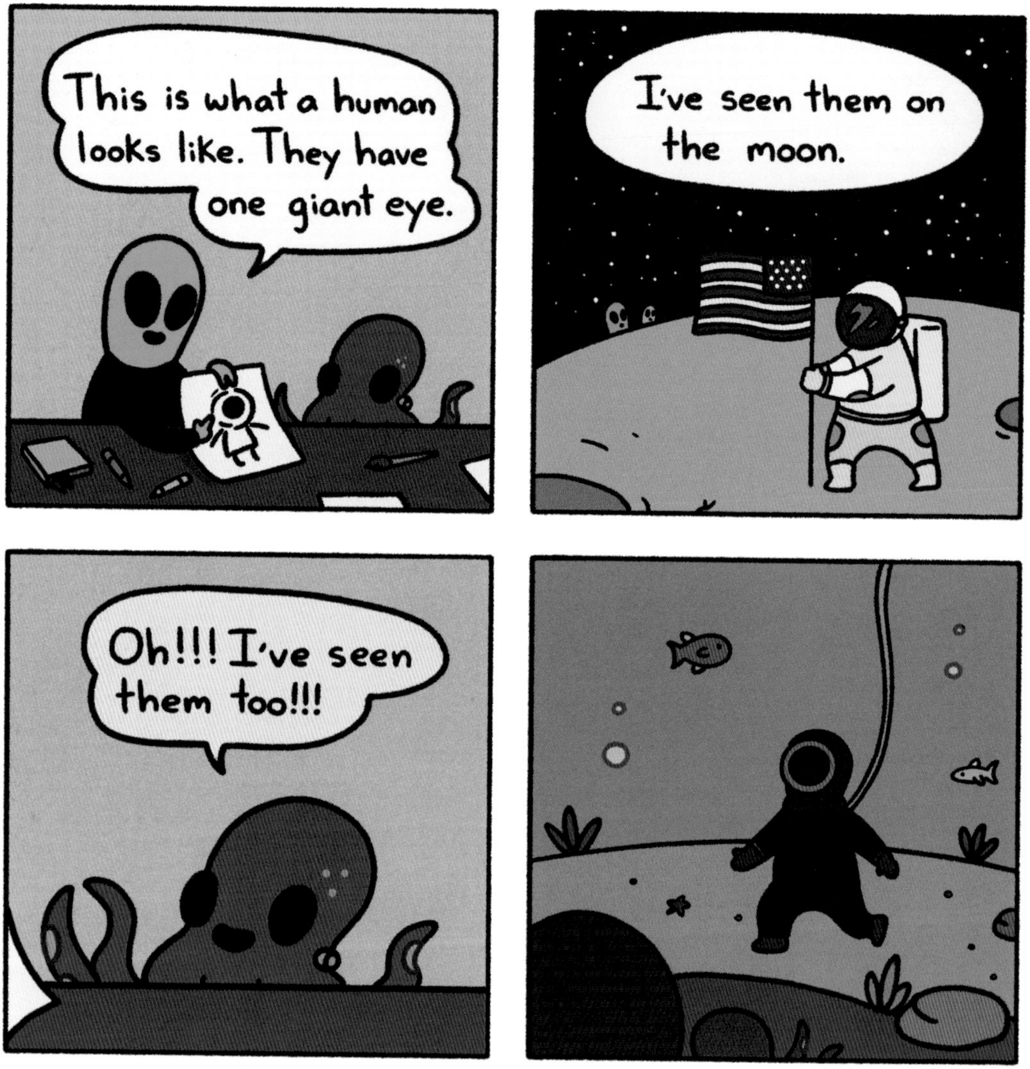
This is what a human looks like. They have one giant eye.
I've seen them on the moon.
Oh!!! I've seen them too!!!

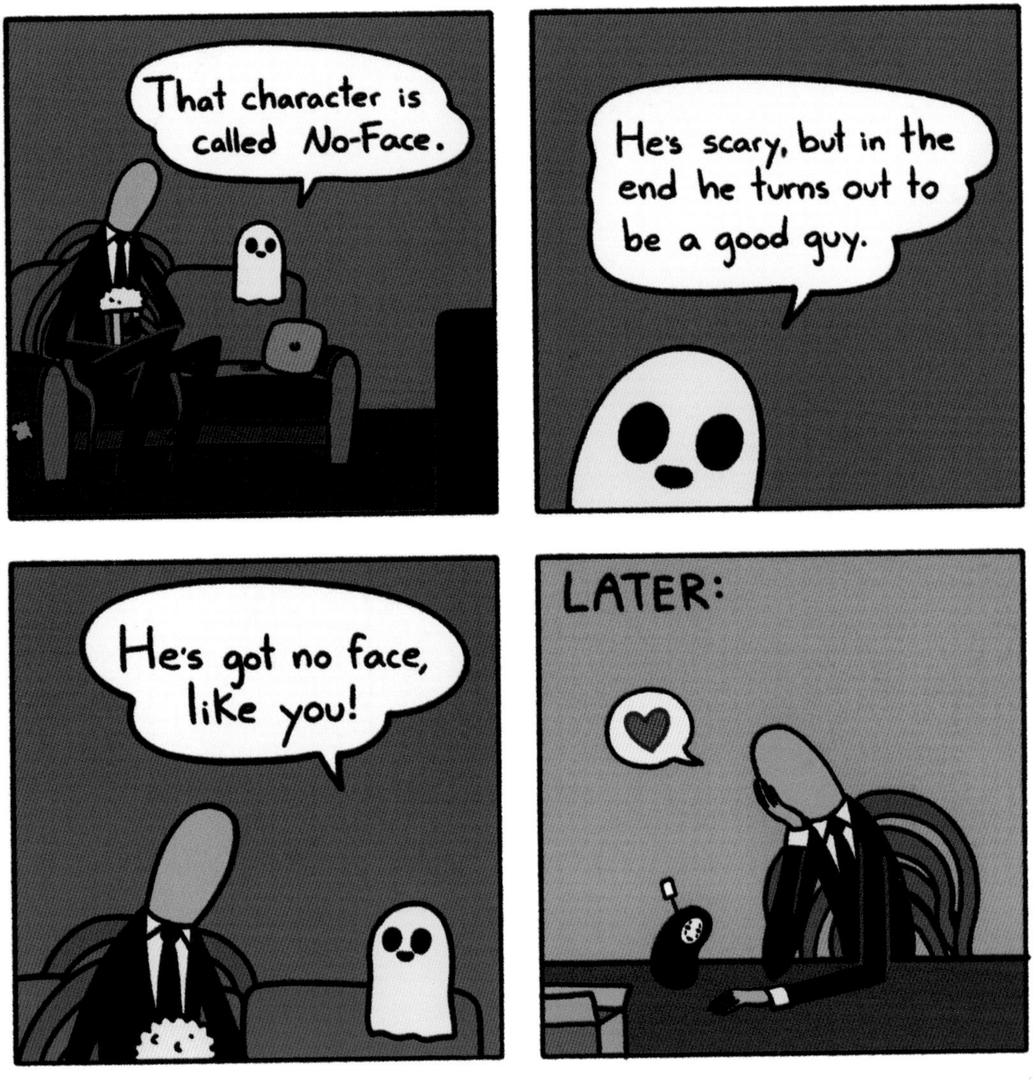
That character is called No-Face.
He's scary, but in the end he turns out to be a good guy.
He's got no face, like you!
LATER:

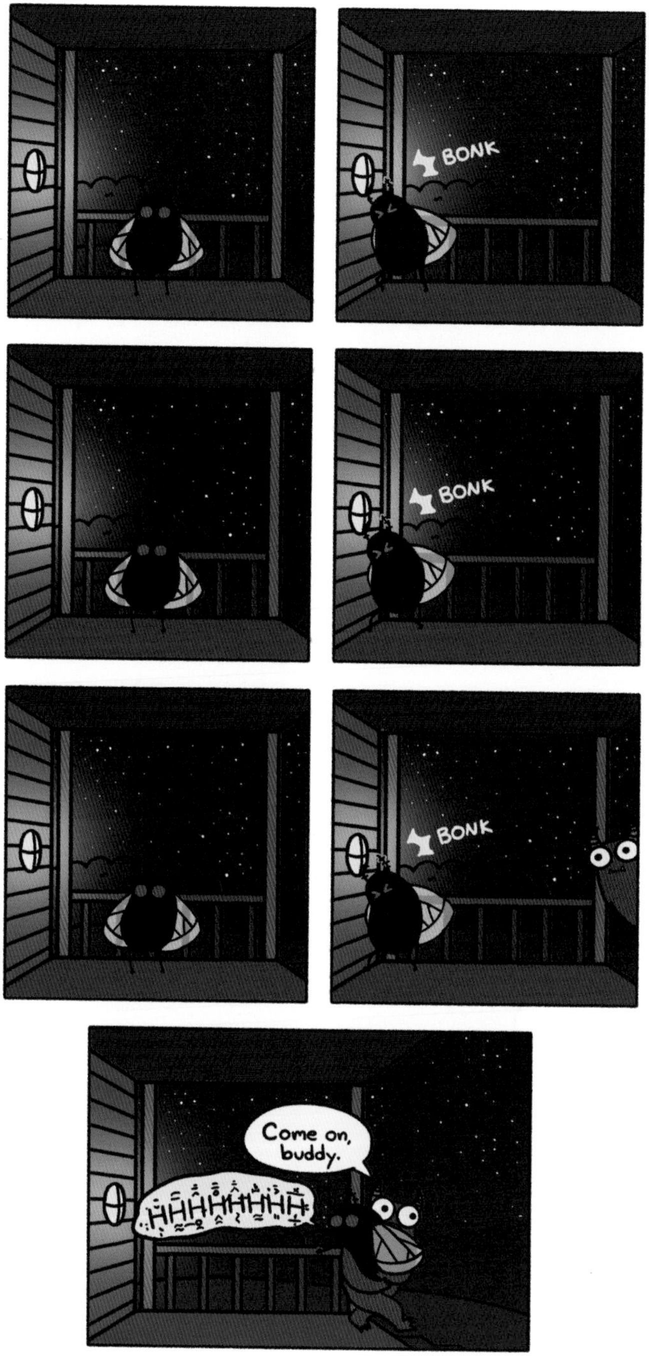
BONK
BONK
BONK
HHHHHHHHHH
Come on, buddy.

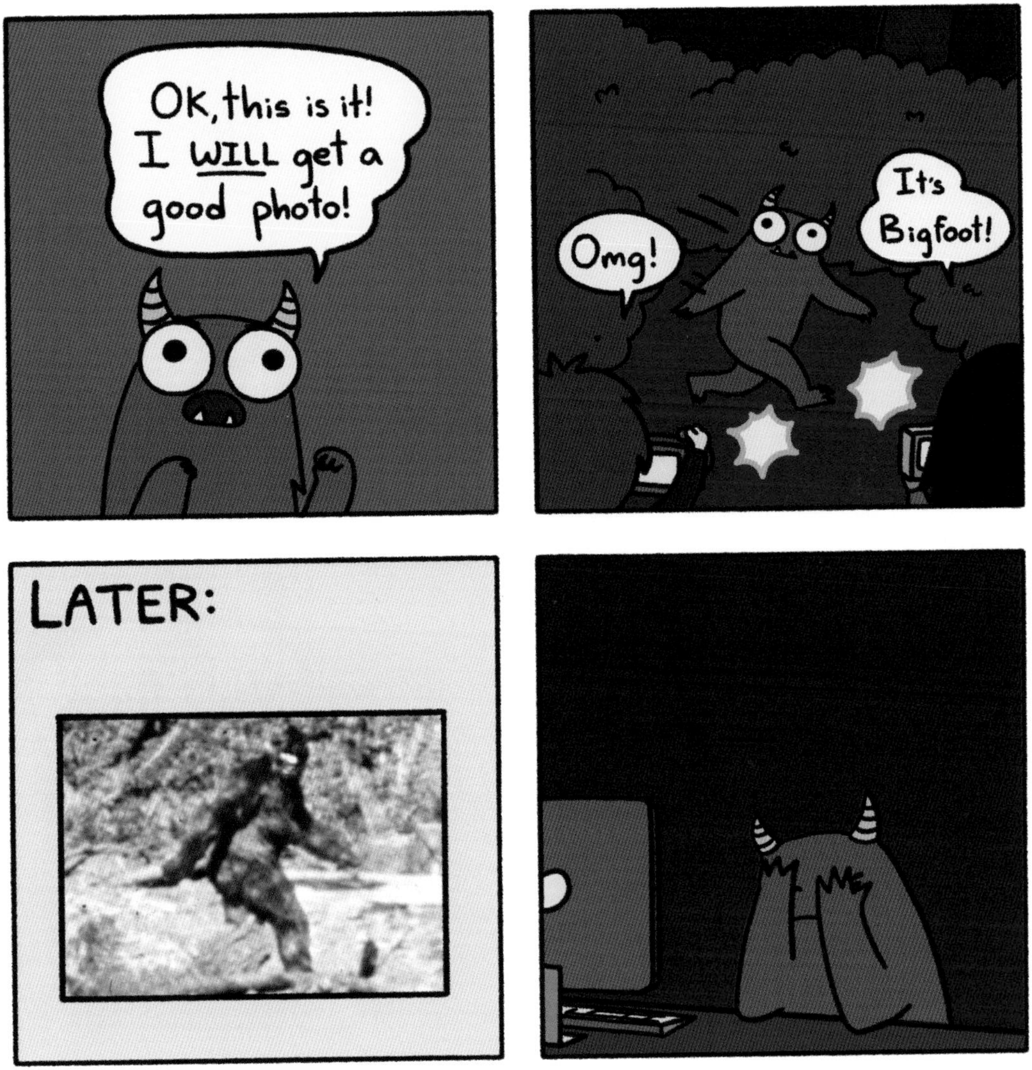
Ok, this is it! I WILL get a good photo!
Omg!
It's Bigfoot!
LATER:

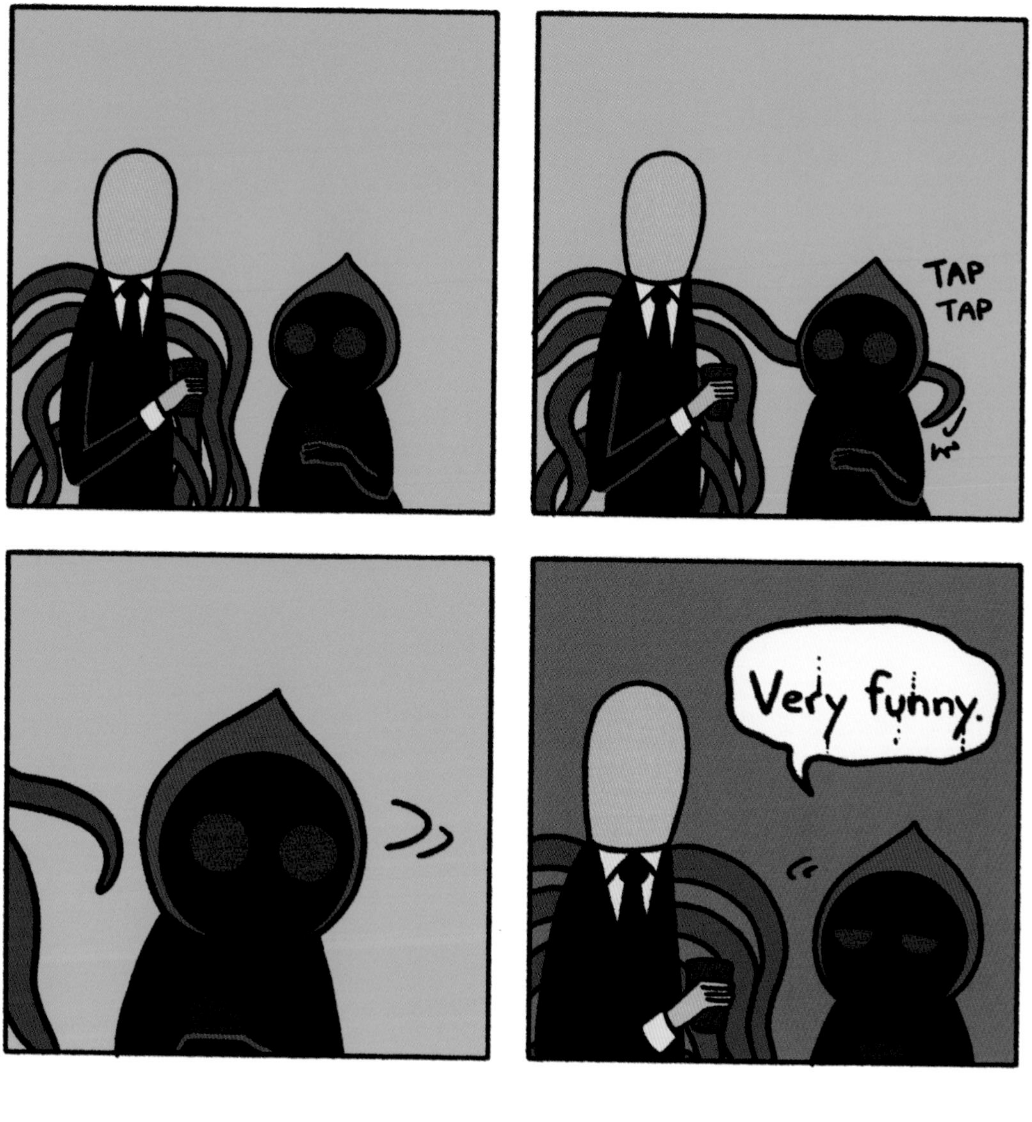
TAP
TAP
Very funny.

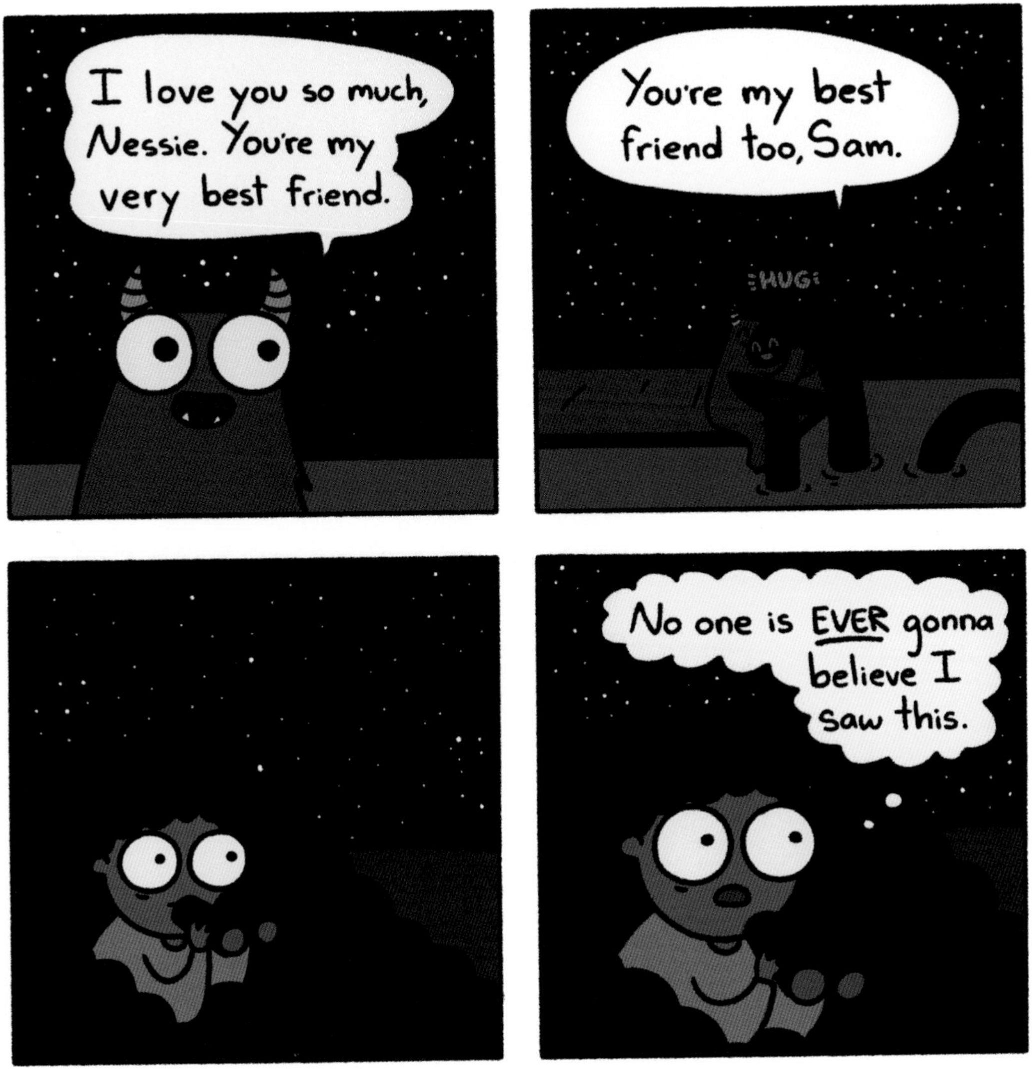
I love you so much, Nessie. You're my very best friend.
You're my best friend too, Sam.
HUG
No one is EVER gonna believe I saw this.

GROUP PHOTO

GLOSSARY

BIGFOOT

Known to roam the forests of North America, Bigfoot is an apelike cryptid who is often spotted in the Pacific Northwest. Lore surrounding a mysterious forest ape has existed for thousands of years, though the Bigfoot name dates back only to the 1950s, when observers were taken aback by the size of his footprints.

CHUPACABRA

Chupacabra can literally be translated as the "goat sucker." Originally from Puerto Rico, this vampiric cryptid is said to terrorize livestock by drinking their blood. He has been described as both reptilian and doglike in appearance.

CLASSIC GHOST

Ghosts have likely been around as long as humans, as they are the souls of those of us who haven't yet crossed over to the other side. Reasons for staying Earth-side include watching over loved ones, unfinished business, or just plain ol' procrastination.

CTHULHU

Part octopus, part dragon, and part human, Cthulhu first appeared in 1928 in the short story "The Call of Cthulhu" by H. P. Lovecraft. Perhaps the most well known of Lovecraft's creatures, Cthulhu is considered a dormant god who haunts humanity's subconscious.

EXTRATERRESTRIALS

Reports of flying saucers started to boom in the 1950s, and little green men have been sighted sporadically ever since. But no one quite knows how long extraterrestrials have been watching mankind; we do know they like to be the observer and not the observed.

FLATWOODS MONSTER

The Flatwoods Monster was first spotted during the 1950s in West Virginia. She has been described as a massive humanoid with glowing red eyes. Though she somewhat resembles a witch, the Flatwoods Monster is suspected to be a misunderstood extraterrestrial.

FRESNO NIGHTCRAWLERS

The Fresno Nightcrawlers started taking strolls past California surveillance cameras during the 2000s. No one quite knows what they are, but some guesses include ghosts; aliens; or walking, haunting pants.

JACKALOPE

The Jackalope has the body of a rabbit but the antlers of a deer, making this cryptid a particularly charming interspecies hybrid. Jackalopes are a popular feature on taxidermy mounts, though one can't imagine they're too thrilled about that.

KRAKEN

The bane of sailors everywhere, the Kraken is known for targeting ships and dragging them all the way to the ocean floor since the thirteenth century. You don't want to get caught in his tentacles.

LOCH NESS MONSTER

The Loch Ness Monster, often affectionately dubbed "Nessie," was first brought to public attention in the 1930s through a series of blurry black-and-white photographs taken at Loch Ness, Scotland. She is said to resemble a plesiosaur, but even with her large stature, she seems to be particularly good at evading sonar.

MOTHMAN

Mothman was first spotted in the Point Pleasant area of West Virginia in 1966, when a couple reported seeing a "man-sized bird . . . creature . . . something." He is known for his signature bright-red glowing eyes as well as his ability to foresee disastrous events.

SIREN

Tales of sirens date back to some of the very first writings in human history. In Greek mythology, they were described as winged, birdlike creatures, but they have since taken on various forms in folklore. They currently present as half-fish, half-human, and 100 percent deadly, as they're known to use their beautiful singing voice to lure in lonely sailors.

SIREN HEAD

Siren Head is a modern cryptid created by horror artist Trevor Henderson in 2018. Siren Head's eerie wails immediately captivated people, and he has been haunting various corners of the Internet ever since.

SLEEP PARALYSIS DEMON

Another cryptid that has likely been with humanity since ancient times, the Sleep Paralysis Demon visits almost half of all people in their lifetime. His visits are usually accompanied by full-body paralysis and an overwhelming sense of dread and terror.

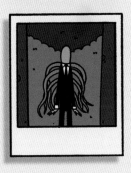

SLENDER MAN

Slender Man is a modern cryptid created by Eric Knudsen in 2009. Depicted as a tall, faceless man in a black suit, Slender Man often makes unexpected appearances in the background of photographs and videos. He is an adept stalker and is known to lure children into the forest with him.

ACKNOWLEDGMENTS

Colors by Céli Godfried
pianta.mystrikingly.com

Flats by Kayla Nicole
@grandmaironlung

Brainstorming help from
Jonathan Kunz
warandpeas.com

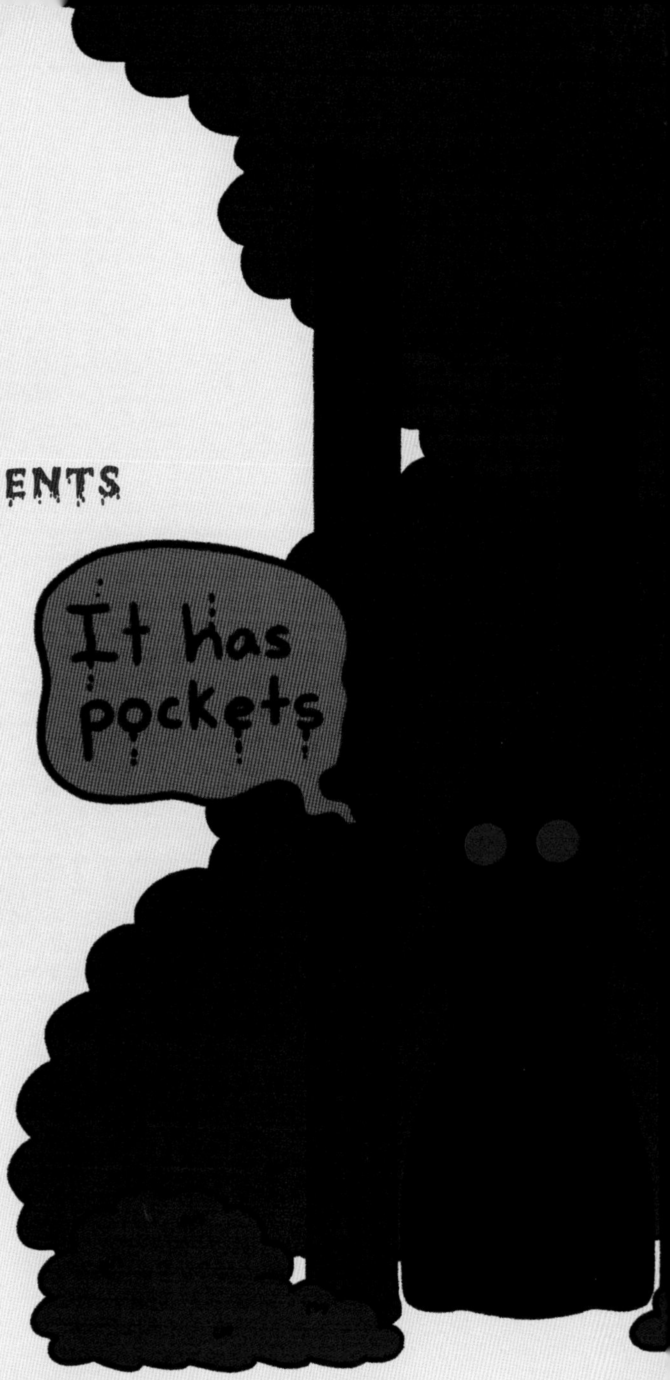
It has pockets

Andrews McMeel Publishing
a division of Andrews McMeel Universal
1130 Walnut Street, Kansas City, Missouri 64106

www.andrewsmcmeel.com

22 23 24 25 26 SDB 10 9 8 7 6 5 4 3 2 1

ISBN: 978-1-5248-7554-1

Library of Congress Control Number: 2021952351

Editor: Lucas Wetzel
Art Director: Diane Marsh
Production Editor: Elizabeth A. Garcia
Production Manager: Tamara Haus

ATTENTION: SCHOOLS AND BUSINESSES
Andrews McMeel books are available at quantity discounts with bulk purchase for educational, business, or sales promotional use. For information, please e-mail the Andrews McMeel Publishing Special Sales Department: specialsales@amuniversal.com.

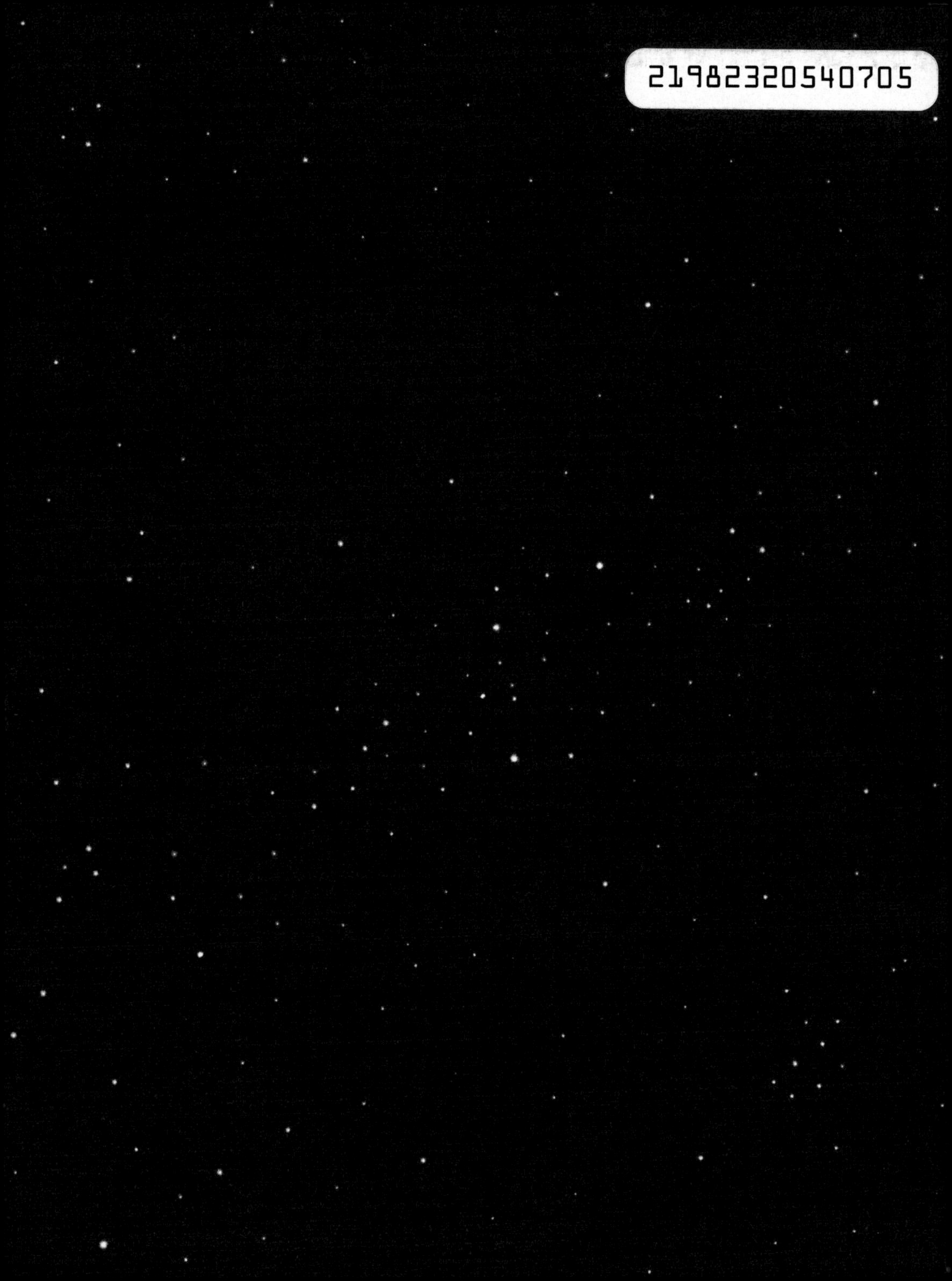